Pitfalls and Planning in Student Teaching

Pitfalls and Planning in Student Teaching

John Heywood

Kogan Page, London
Nichols Publishing Company, New York

First published in Great Britain in 1982
by Kogan Page Ltd, 120 Pentonville Road, London N1 9JN

Copyright © 1982 John Heywood
British Library Cataloguing in Publication Data

Heywood, John, *1930—*
    Pitfalls and planning in student teaching.
    1. Teaching
    I. Title
    371.1'02   L1025.Z

ISBN 0-85038-554-7

First published in the USA by Nichols Publishing Company,
PO Box 96, New York, NY10024

Library of Congress Cataloging in Publication Data

Pitfalls and planning in student teaching.

    1. Student teaching.   2. Lesson planning.
    I. Heywood, John, 1930—
    LB2157.A3P5   1982   370'.7'33   82-3555
    ISBN 0-89397-133-2   AACR2

Printed in Great Britain by The Anchor Press Ltd
and bound by Wm Brendon and Son Ltd,
both of Tiptree, Essex

Contents

Preface

The student teachers for whom I am responsible teach in their second level schools throughout the school year. During the University's academic terms they teach in the mornings, and undertake their educational studies in the University in the afternoons. In this way, despite the strain, we hope there will be an integration between theory and practice.

Because schools start in the first week of September we run an induction course during that month, partly to provide the students with a 'survival kit' for their classroom experiences, and partly to prepare them for some of the courses which lie ahead.

Last year, on the first day of the induction course, the booksellers told us that the two books which we normally used were not available, despite the fact that they had been ordered four months previously. One we were told was out of print, and the publishers sent us an inspection copy of a possible alternative. It did not meet our requirements as the other text had done, and in a fit of pique I told the publishers that I would write one myself. However, when I came to look at the problem it seemed to me that to try to write a cheap edition about all the work which has been done in educational research would be wasteful repetition; students could use the library copies of the more expensive texts. What was wanted was something based primarily on the experience of student teachers during their first year of teaching which, while being a component of the survival kit, would also prepare them for the courses to come and, more especially, introduce them to some of the language used in educational studies.

The structure of the text borrows heavily from D P Ausubel's idea of the 'advanced organizer'. Chapter 1 on advanced organization explains this concept. This chapter also makes use of this idea in its structure, for which reason it begins with illustrations of examination questions and quotations from student responses to them. The immediate relevance of these may not be apparent to the reader; but they are intended to set the scene for what follows.

Later chapters are structured in the same way. The opening sections of each chapter consist of an examination question or questions which relate to the themes in the chapter, and are followed by extracts from students' answers to these questions in their final examination papers. They are presented by kind permission of the students concerned. Please remember that they were written under the pressure of examination conditions: we do not expect perfection in such responses and I have made no attempt to edit them. Their inclusion does not necessarily imply that I agree with what is said; their purposes are, as is explained in Chapter 1, to act as advanced organizers and to illustrate students' experiences.

J Heywood
Dublin, January 1982

Acknowledgements

I am very grateful to the Higher Diploma students of the 1980-81 year at the University of Dublin Department of Teacher Education for allowing me to quote from their examination scripts. They would doubtless wish to revise them with hindsight, and readers should remember that they were written under the pressure of examination conditions.

The following have contributed to this study: E Altman; O M Bodell; A J L Bolt; C Breathnach; P Bugwandeen; N Carson; G Cashel; F Claffey; H Conway; C J Copeland; B F Dagg; M Deasy; M Devlin; C Doyle; D J Duffy; C Edge; G P Edgill; P N Fanning; A B Farrell; K L Felber; M F Fennell; P Fitzsimmons; L A C Gault; E Hargaden; J R Hartnett; J P B Hollwey; M F Jennings; J Johnson; K Maume; P E McCarthy; J McCormack; M K McSkane; M Miller; B P Montague; K F Murray; D Nolan; J P O'Brien; F O'Byrne; E M O'Connell; M O'Connor; F O'Leary; M O'Rourke; M O'Sullivan; P G M O'Sullivan; A Pearson-Evans; A E Potter; B A Sweeney; S E Townsend; P Trewhela; M B Walsh; A Webb; H M Wynne. Thanks also to those who have contributed from other courses, Karen Goodbody and Gina Plunkett.

I am grateful to David Heywood for typing the manuscript in time for it to be available for the 1981-82 course, and to Miss Janet Monaghan who subsequently undertook the typing of the revisions with the help of the Secretary to the Department of Teacher Education, Miss Elizabeth Fleeton.

1 Advanced Organization

1.1 Some advanced organizers

Describe two kinds of advanced organizer for use in learning the same material in the subject which you teach. Indicate the characteristics of those advanced organizers and say why you think they will facilitate the acquisition of new information. *Examination question modified from one in McDonald (1968)*

No work has been set, no relationship established, no link formed to previous lessons to aid memory recall, no exposition of the objective of the lesson (Ausubel has sunk without trace — 'advance organizers' have never reached Mr X's ears). *From a student's response to the question on discipline at the beginning of Chapter 2*

Ausubel also postulates advance organizers: a theory I tested with my fourth class history lessons on St Colmcille. After a brief introduction half the class read the account of his life in the history book, with a view to answering questions on it. The other half had to write the answers to four key questions on the life of Colmcille. Thus while reading they were searching for the answers to these questions which were keys to his life-story. They acted as sorting categories into which they could fit the rest of the information, and this task was a preparation for the major learning task: ability to reproduce eight facts on St Colmcille's life. Those guided by the written questions retained significantly more. *From a student's response to the examination question discussed in section 1.3*

Ausubel has also his part to offer in the educational process. His approach would lie somewhere between Gagné's and Bruner's work. He sees the need for 'advance organizers'. Here ideas are presented to the pupils which will prepare them for what is to be learned. Ausubel gave various groups material about metals in preparation for a class on these metals. Some groups only received information on the history of the metals while others were given information more relevant to the new lesson. It was found that these profited greatly from having been introduced to the 'advance organizers' and achieved more as a result. I have used advance organizers in my own class of third year pupils. They were introduced to new words in Irish before being presented with one of the stories on the Intermediate Cert course which they were required to read. On a subsequent occasion my class was split because of Christmas examinations. One group received instruction by means of the 'advance organizers'. The other group did not. Instead they were given a brief summary of the story. The group using the 'advance organizers' were superior to the other group when tested on the contents of the story. *From a student's response to the examination question discussed in section 1.2*

1.2 Advanced organizers

Advanced organizers are a form of mediating response. Their intention is to facilitate meaningful learning. As the term 'advanced' suggests, they precede a major learning task although they are a learning task themselves.

D P Ausubel, who was responsible for this idea, uses concepts and principles to help the further explanation and organization of a more substantial body of material on the same subject. In this way both readiness and structure are provided.

Most textbooks cite two examples from early papers by Ausubel. The first relates to the teaching of the metallurgical properties of plain carbon steel and the second to Buddhism and Zen Buddhism. In both cases experimental and control groups were used and pre- and post-tests given. The differences in the treatment between the experimental and control groups were in the type of advanced organizer they were given. Figure 1.1 shows my interpretation of the arrangement of the experiment which is in the traditional form of a scientific experiment. The same post-test was, of course, set to both groups. The most successful of the two was the experimental group in which the advanced organizer contained basic principles.

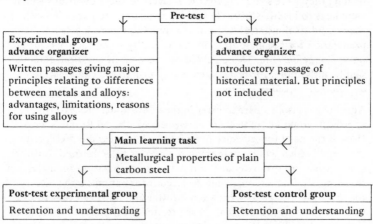

Figure 1.1

One way in which to learn both complex and simple things is by similarity and differences. If we want to remember the differences between two theories we try to understand the ways in which their basic parameters differ. The degree of contrast may be important. This is illustrated by Ausubel's experiment with Buddhism in which the respondents were to distinguish between Buddhist and Zen Buddhist doctrines. Once again, a pre-test for prior knowledge was given. The experimental technique is shown in Figure 1.2.

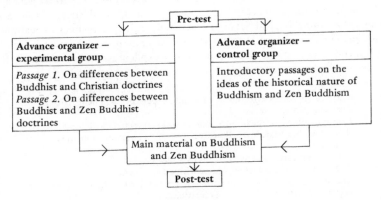

Figure 1.2

Although the experimental group did better than the control group it was in respect of Buddhism; neither group did so well on Zen Buddhism. Ausubel has suggested that there were difficulties in discriminating between the two forms of Buddhism. The questions in the post-test were multiple choice, and we know little of how people respond in these situations to different types of test. If they had to write an essay on the two forms of Buddhism, their understanding of the differences might have been different. Be that as it may, the effects of advanced organizers on learning have been consistently obtained.

The examples from student responses to examination questions and the examination question which preceded this section are forms of advanced organization, in that they focus on the problem to be studied. The examination question is more a statement of objectives than an advanced organizer, since it does not state any principles. It focuses on the issue to be discussed and indicates the significant element — the characteristics which the student should understand. You may say that the examples of student responses do not really describe these characteristics of advanced organizers, or that they suggest that every kind of material will be successful. You may feel that advanced organizers will not work with children who are not capable of Piaget's stage of formal operations. But if the organizers in this chapter have stimulated you to read on, then they will have achieved some of their purpose. If the organizers suggest that the structure of the content and its presentation in the first phase of your lessons influences the way in which your pupils respond, a little more will have been achieved. If you are motivated to experiment with advanced organizers in your classes, so much the better!

1.3 Advanced organizers and other principles of learning

Advanced organizers contribute to effective learning in two important respects. First, since learning is that process by which experience develops new and reorganizes old concepts, the organizers provide a link between the old and the new. Second, advanced organizers contribute to transfer by providing meaning, structure and organization. That advanced organizers can aid learning is clear from the generally agreed principles of learning outlined in Exhibit 1.1. (This Exhibit has some of the characteristics of advanced organization, since implicit and explicit references are made to these principles throughout the book.)

---

1. Without appropriate readiness a learning experience will be inefficient. Learning may not occur.
2. Learning proceeds much more rapidly and is retained much longer when that which has to be learned possesses meaning, organization and structure.
3. The learner learns only what he himself does.
4. Only those responses which are confirmed are learned.
5. Transfer can only occur when there is a recognized similarity between the learning situation and the transfer situation.
6. Transfer will occur to the extent that students expect it to occur.
7. Knowledge of a model of problem solving or aspects of critical thinking can contribute to its improvement.

Exhibit 1.1 *Some generally agreed principles of learning (after J L Saupé)*

The advanced organizer is a sorting and classifying mechanism. Ausubel writes:

Logically meaningful material becomes incorporated most readily and stably in cognitive structure in so far as it is subsumable under specifically relevant existing ideas. It follows, therefore, that increasing the availability in cognitive structure of specifically relevant subsumers — by emplanting suitable organizers — should enhance the meaningful learning of such material. (Ausubel, 1968: p 137)

In a later passage he lists the components of the rationale as follows:

(a) the importance of having relevant and otherwise appropriate established ideas *already* available in cognitive structure to make logically meaningful new ideas potentially meaningful and to give them stable anchorage; (b) the advantages of using the more general and inclusive ideas or subsumers (namely, the aptness and specificity of their relevance, their greater inherent stability, their greater explanatory power, and their integrative capacity); and (c) the fact that they themselves attempt both to identify already existing relevant content in cognitive structure (and to be explicitly related to it) and to indicate explicitly both the relevance of the latter content and their own relevance for the new learning material. *In short, the principal function of the organizer is to bridge the gap between what the learner already knows and what he needs to know before he can successfully learn the task at hand.* (Ausubel, 1968: p 138)

Ausubel's description is in a much more technical language than the descriptions of his work by such authors as Biehler (1978: p 427), De Cecco and Crawford (1974: pp 339-40) or McDonald (1968: pp 223-4). But the previous discussion of the idea may have acted as an advanced organizer for some readers of this material. More recent research has suggested that the student needs to be capable of formal operations, or in Bruner's term the symbolic mode of thought. This suggests that the advanced organizer should be a quite useful technique in the later stages of second level education.

Good teachers probably use organizers without needing to be told that educational research has found that in certain circumstances and with certain types of learner they are effective. Nevertheless, it is clear that certain types of advanced organizer do not work. As the example at the beginning of the chapter shows, it should be possible for the student teacher to organize a simple experiment to test the efficacy of different kinds of organizers among the pupils he or she teaches.

1.4 Mediating responses

As we saw above, learning is that process by which experience develops new responses and reorganizes old ones. There is, therefore, a connection between that which is already learned and that which is intended to be learned. At the same time, we require some stimuli to learn.

Without any knowledge of educational psychology, teachers use these principles to aid learning, through the association of one idea with another. To do this they use a *mediating response*, ie a term in the form:

- is like,
- is different from.

Using statements which include these terms, new phenomena or things can be related to the experience of the pupil. However, mediating responses have to be used with care: they may cause ambiguity, or they may not be understood. For example, McDonald (1968) points out that teachers sometimes use the word *familiar* instead of *experience*. They also use *familiarity* in two different senses. Great care must be exercised in the choice of such terms to ensure that they are clearly understood by the students in the context in which they are to be used. Mediating responses like 'is different from' may also cause the teacher considerable problems since the pupils may not grasp the significant differences; here the teacher is likely to be helped by the research which has been done on concept learning (see Chapter 5).

1.5 Other kinds of advanced organizer

Ausubel pointed out that textbooks can be structured so that in the first half of the book there is discussion of the essential principles which will be used to organize the material in the second half of the book. He cites as an example Boyd's *Textbook on Pathology*.

There is no doubt that pupils and teachers have difficulty with some of their textbooks: some mathematics texts in particular are very bad. Sometimes teachers are forced to write their own notes. One of our students showed how she used the principle of advanced organization to rectify difficulties promoted by the textbook thus:

> I have used Ausubel's theory of instruction in my own classroom. He advocates the use of advanced organizers. I had begun human (reproduction) biology and was about to teach the digestive system. I realized that all the books would be using terms like enzymes and starch, proteins and vitamins. Before introducing digestion we had a lesson on diet and the seven types of food used in daily diet. This was a form of advanced organizer and I used it to facilitate the learning of the digestive system. It was a stepping stone to digestion . . .

We often provide prior information to facilitate learning but such information is not an advanced organizer. For example, a statement of objectives for a lesson will give some meaning, organization and structure to the lesson. Statements of objectives for a whole course do not seem to have much conscious impact on student learning, whereas question spotting from previous papers does. I use examination questions quite specifically to try to make students relate theory to practice. Contrast the form of the examination question at the beginning of this chapter with its original form which read as follows:

> Construct at least two kinds of advanced organizers for use in learning the same material. Indicate the characteristics of the advanced organizers and why you think they will facilitate acquiring new information.

The former insists that respondents give examples from their own teaching, whereas responses to the latter could come from examples in a textbook.

In my book on *Examining in Second Level Education* I have argued that examination questions are valuable because they help students integrate their learning and experience as they relate to a variety of teaching situations. The examples in this chapter came from responses to questions other than those set directly on advanced organizers, which suggests that the students were integrating the disparately presented ideas in the course into coherent components of their teaching.

Examinations provide extrinsic motivation. Advanced organizers must also influence motivation. Motivation will be considered more fully in Chapter 3: for the time being, we will consider the case where the examination questions are given in advance ('prior-notice questions' as they are sometimes called). This technique can lead to an improvement in examination performance, and I use it quite regularly both to encourage and to direct reading. A list of questions with directions for associated reading is given to the students at the beginning of the year. The examination paper contains three, perhaps four, questions from this list, which have to be answered. The questions enshrine the objectives of the course.

1.6 Aims and objectives of this book

As has already been explained, the purpose of this book is to provide information to student teachers which is likely to be helpful to them in the planning and implementation of lessons. The opening sections of each chapter consist of an examination question or questions which relate to the themes of the chapter, and which I hope will induce students to think about the relationship between theory and practice. The questions are followed, as in this chapter, by extracts from students' answers to these questions. The same principle is thus being used as that used on our course described above.

But there are two aims which will not be dealt with anywhere else but here. The first is that the student should develop his own learning theory which he can defend. In the past I have asked students to discuss the merits of this view in examination questions. Most recently I asked the following:

> 'Education is necessarily an eclectic subject.' Discuss this statement
> with reference to the contrasting theories of instruction of Bruner,
> Gagné and Ausubel and their application to your work in the classroom.

This should force the candidate to indicate his own views. Questions of this kind can only be answered after the teacher training course has been completed: nevertheless, during the course students should focus their minds on the development of an adequate theory of learning.

The second all-embracing aim is to encourage every teacher to undertake research on his classroom activities. I once set the following examination question to see if this goal had been achieved:

> 'Teaching is a continuing process of educational research.' Discuss this
> statement with reference to any experiment published by a research
> worker which you have tested or will test with your pupils.

Some weeks prior to the examination I issued an example of educational research in the classroom. It related to the teaching of cognitive dissonance in the teaching of politics (see Chapter 4). The paper was accompanied by a note to the effect that this was a good example of the kind of enquiry which a teacher could conduct in the classroom. But no explanation of research techniques was given; neither did I provide simple illustrations. I had done this in previous years but had not set an examination question with this motif.

An example of the kind of investigation which can be done by the teacher in the classroom is to be found in Bruner's *The Process of Education*. He describes an investigation by Patrick Suppes who while observing mathematics teaching found that the form $3 + \underline{x} = 8$ was easier for children to deal with than the form $\underline{x} + 3 = 8$. Several explanations are offered as to why this might be. The point is that observations which lead to generalizable conclusions about one's teaching can lead to important modifications in technique and presentation. One of my experienced teacher friends came up with some interesting findings on the influence of mathematical technique on the understanding of physical problems (Heywood, 1976). Evidently high powered mathematics could impede understanding of the physical principles involved.

A student respondent in an examination answer gave this example of an experiment:

> I tried an experiment on my second year 'homogeneous' class. The subjects I chose were maths and science (I teach mainly science). Having only known these children for less than a year I found it very difficult to assess their abilities in maths and science. I looked up their marks in both subjects for the time they had been in secondary school. I paid particular attention to any tests or examinations which I had given to them. I consulted their previous science teacher and their past and present maths teacher for their impressions. I found myself being very influenced by other people's impressions and my own which may have been misleading. I then deduced what I thought were three groups — a success, a failure and a mixed. I gave everyone a maths problem, he estimated how he would do and then did it. He was then given another maths problem, having been told whether he was right or wrong. Everyone was given in total five maths problems. In the same way each was given five scientific tasks to perform. These tasks were very varied — involved drawing something from a microscope slide, measuring the density of an object.
>
> I found in general that those who were successful at maths were successful in the maths side of science. There were others who were unsuccessful in maths but successful in the more 'biological', less mathematical side of science.

As the advanced organizer and this illustration show, student teachers can conduct experiments which are helpful to their teaching. For this a framework of theory is necessary. The chapters which follow aim to provide an illustration to that framework.

References

Advanced organizers

D P Ausubel (1968) *Educational Psychology: A Cognitive View*. New York: Holt, Rinehart and Winston.

B R Barnes and E V Clawson (1975) Do advanced organisers facilitate learning? Recommendations for further research based on 32 studies, *Review of Educational Research*, 45, 637-59.

R F Biehler (1978) *Psychology Applied to Teaching*, 3rd edition. Boston, Mass: Houghton Mifflin.

J P De Cecco and W R Crawford (1974) *The Psychology of Learning and Instruction*. Englewood Cliffs, NJ: Prentice-Hall.

F J McDonald (1968) *Educational Psychology*. Belmont, Cal: Wadsworth.

Other references

J Bruner (1960) *The Process of Education*. Cambridge, Mass: Harvard University Press.

J Heywood (1978) *Examining in Second Level Education*. Dublin: Association of Secondary Teachers, Ireland.

J L Saupé (1961) in P Dressel (ed) *Evaluation in Higher Education*. Boston, Mass: Houghton Mifflin.

On mathematics and the learning of physics:

J Heywood (1976) *Assessment in Mathematics (Twelve to Fifteen)*. P74 Dublin, Second Report of the Public Examinations Evaluation Project, School of Education, University of Dublin.

On classroom research:

E Stones (1979) *Psychopedagogics*. London: Methuen.

For more detailed illustrations:

J Clement (1981) Solving problems with formulas: some limitations, *Journal of Engineering Education*, 72 (2), 158-62.

2 Discipline

. . . all teachers realize the need for discipline of one sort or another and this was the biggest source of conversation in the staff room I was in last year. What to do with X or how best to solve the problem of Y.
In a student response to an examination question

2.1 Introduction and note on additional reading

The two problems which seem to bother students most before they take their first class are those of discipline and motivation, which is why this text begins with commentaries on these two issues. 'How shall I cope if a pupil answers me back?' 'What shall I do if they get bored and start messing about?' These are but two of the questions which run through a student teacher's mind the night before he is due to take his first class.

By the time students come to our induction course they will have had experience of six or more sessions with a class. They will have acquired a framework with which to ask questions of experienced teachers. So a session is arranged with teachers of considerable repute who are known to be effective teachers in the classroom. Our annual feedback sessions always tell us that the students feel that neither in the induction course, nor in the courses proper, is there sufficient discussion of the problem of discipline. It is also evident that the reading on this area is much thumbed by the time they come to the induction course. Had I not inspected many examination papers I would not have expected theory to inform practice: however, there is considerable evidence in the answers to examination questions to show that the reading was helpful and influenced their behaviour.

The recommended reading for the induction course is:

K Barnes (1966) *Involved Man — Action and Reflection in the Life of a Teacher.* London: National Children's Home.

L Cohen and L Mannion (1977) *A Guide to Teaching Practice.* London: Methuen.

J W Docking (1980) *Control and Discipline in Schools: Perspectives and Approaches.* London: Harper and Row.

Mention should be made of the fact that these three books are by English authors. Although they make use of much American and British research it always needs to be remembered that attitudes to discipline and classroom behaviour are very much peculiar both to the culture and the particular school in which the teacher finds him or herself in that culture.

Finally, it is worth noting in this introductory section that all the traditional subjects of the educational curriculum have something of value to contribute to discipline and its handling in schools. In the sections which follow, therefore, there will be examples which impinge on the philosophy of education, the psychology of learning, and the sociology of knowledge.

The answers in the sections which follow were written in response to the following questions:

(1) 'The perception that a teacher has of his role in the classroom will determine his views of the aims of discipline.' Discuss.

(2) 'Mr X has a second year D stream class of boys. He enters the classroom which is untidy, with papers scattered on the floor. He checks at random a few exercise copies. On checking Raymond's exercise he finds it to be untidy, and comments, "Knowing you, and where you come from, what could I expect?"'

'Very few students have attempted their homework. The teacher orders the entire class to stay in during lunch. While the teacher works at the chalkboard he hears students talk. He turns and orders Raymond outside the door. The Principal meets Raymond and orders him back into class. At this stage the teacher orders this student to the corner of the room for the remainder of the class.' (Clar do Mhunttgoiri Nuacheaptha, 1979)

Discuss the actions of the teacher indicating what you feel their effect will be (a) on the immediate problem and (b) on the teacher's relationship with the class. Make reference to any theoretical studies on discipline you have read.

2.2 The aims of discipline and the structure of knowledge

(a) Five extracts from answers to question (1) above

1. In the past discipline derived from the following of someone or some ideal: one became a disciple. In order to be a disciple a certain order and commitment was required. This order and commitment was related to some clearly accepted ideal or person. Today the issue is complicated by the fact that in many schools of the Western world no such ideal or person is accepted. Discipline only has real meaning as providing some order to attain an accepted value. Our values today compete for acceptance. Tension is created by the imposition of a meaningless order, ie an order which leads to no universally accepted goal. Many factors influence this lack of harmony in regard to value acceptance and they are not necessarily bad.

2. Barnes' theory of discipline indicated that it should be a means to an end and that if it became an end in itself it would become educationally dangerous. This view of discipline always kept the aim in view. He said that much discipline resulted from fear — fear of the dark side of the human personality. The teacher should realize that selfishness, quarrelling, etc are part of the child's nature and that he should regard them as the nature of the material he is dealing with. Sensitivity of the teacher to when the child may be led from this particular phase and when he may need help and encouragement was very important.

3. Up until recently, the traditional teacher-centred approach to teaching insisted on the children being passive receivers and the teacher being the active agent. That system emphasized the need for *control* — and even in modern language teaching classes, children were to be subjected to an audio-lingual method, which again insisted on them listening passively, repeating without thought, not speaking until they had been spoken to, etc.

   Happily there is a tendency now — especially with the inset of audiovisual courses and the notional/functional courses in particular — to get the children to *participate* in the class, to do things, eg role-playing, simulation games, etc. The modern language teacher, far from suppressing free expression is encouraged to stimulate the students to *speak* in the classroom — among themselves, in groups, etc.[1]

4. What does one mean when one says the role of the teacher? It seems to me that a teacher's perception of his role in the classroom is occasionally affected by the aims and objectives he has for teaching. For instance he could see his role as the development in his pupils of the higher order cognitive activities of analysis, synthesis and evaluation. In other words he would see the development of the students' critical faculties as his main aim and would probably tend to see the subject material used to develop these qualities as to a degree arbitrary and definitely not fixed.

   Another teacher might see the transfer of a written body of knowledge to his students as his essential role. He would see teaching as more vocational in nature and believe it necessary for his students to be able to take their place in society in some specific way. For this he would regard a certain core curriculum as being essential. Now these are two sets of aims and objectives which are likely to lead to two different perceptions of role in the classroom.

   The first teacher is more likely to encourage more student-centred activities in the classroom in an attempt to develop the cognitive processes mentioned already, group work being the obvious example. He is also more likely to encourage questions, especially questions about the assumptions he makes and the methods he uses. He is finally more liable to use discovery or guided discovery techniques in teaching and be more concerned with process rather than product. The second teacher's teaching practice is likely to be more teacher-centred. His teaching is likely to be more product oriented and also more dependent on his authority.

5. Does a teacher see his role as that of imposing knowledge on children who have little or any information or does he see his role as one of helping children grow and develop at their own rate? What does a teacher want to do and feel he should do? What are his ideas about readiness? How important are the students? What really is one's role as a teacher? The answers to these questions *determine not just the aims of discipline but the aims of education for him.*

(b) Commentary

(i) SOCIETY AND DISCIPLINE

Most of the essential principles stand out in these advanced organizers. It is evident that attitudes to discipline among pupils have changed in the last 30 years. Prior to the second world war it seems that pupils acquiesced in regimented if not harsh discipline. The great change in education since then seems to have been in the affective domain: the majority of pupils seem to be more articulate and assertive even though they may not know their grammar or their arithmetic. They reflect different social attitudes to both discipline and moral behaviour. Often the teacher is left behind, as in the following example of a teacher speaking to a seven-year-old child about her mother's absence from the teacher-parent evening about the performance of children in the class.

'Where was your mum last night?'
'She had to visit my dad — he's in prison.'
'Oh dear.'
'Yes, dad did another fellah in.'
'Oh . . .'
'But it's all right Miss, my uncle's going to do that chap in tonight for getting my dad in trouble with the police.'

Of course, most teachers do not have to cope with this kind of problem. Nevertheless, many are increasingly finding that the knowledge acquired from their everyday experience does not equip them to cope with the problem with which they are presented. To be faced with a child from a so-called middle-class background who tells an equally middle-class teacher to 'f— off' may pose quite serious problems for that teacher.

There is an onus on every teacher to formulate his value system for it is open to him to influence society through the curriculum offered, his colleagues, parents, and the union to which he belongs. Teachers have in the past tended not to query the curriculum, but to accept it as received wisdom. However, it does not on the surface prepare people for life except in a limited way. For instance, pupils are not, generally, educated to cope with the media, yet television is a powerful mediating force on our values; and the majority of pupils do not receive any specific training for parenthood.

Teachers are obliged to have informed opinions about everything, more especially those things which it is believed that education can solve on behalf of the community as the community sheds its responsibility. Thus we have to acquire a view about the effects of unemployment on the behaviour of children (more especially in the classroom). M Laufer, a psychoanalyst (*The Times*, July 15 1981) wrote:

> The disorder and despair among the young is great not only when they are unemployed and see no change, but when the father shares the despair and humiliation of being made to feel useless. Toxteth, Manchester, Salford, Southall and Brixton may also be expressing the despair and violence of the father via the sons towards a society that has classed them as worthless.

So it is that the value dispositions of teachers are of considerable importance. That is why the courses with which I am associated have considerable components in the philosophy and sociology of education which some students think are too theoretical. We also pay attention to theories of moral education, and in particular to the developmental theory of Kohlberg.[2] Even if we feel that values are a personal matter, they enter into the classroom situation and influence the teacher's attitude to discipline, as the student response below shows:

> The teacher's personal values will also come into play in her perceptions of her classroom role. She may see it as her 'right' to impose discipline in order to enforce the values of society on the class. On the other hand, the teacher with strong Christian values will perceive her rule more on the level of love and acceptance, and will be reluctant to force individuals to do something against their will — for fear of punishment. This does not mean however that the class will go wild; rather a more positive attitude to discipline is taken. Instead of using discipline as a threat as the authoritarian teacher might do, it is used as a positive reinforcer, with encouragement at self-discipline. The teacher may try to encourage this through the lesson content; by making it interesting and lively discipline will be implicit in the class.

(ii) THE AIMS OF DISCIPLINE AND LEARNING
It is clear that the aims which we have for discipline are likely to influence our behaviour in the classroom. It is also clear that the student respondents believe that the aim of discipline is effective learning. If X with the aid of an elastic band is firing paper pellets at Y, then X is interfering with Y's ability to learn. Learning is not promoted through fear.

(iii) DISCIPLINE CURRICULUM; TEACHING STYLE AND ROLE
Three perspectives of the second level curriculum have been distinguished

by sociologists. They are given the terms received, reflexive, and restructured (Eggleston, 1977).[3] They *may* be associated with two kinds of
teaching style — teacher-centred and student-centred. Where there is a
received curriculum as, for example, the curriculum for national schools
(5-12 years) in Ireland, a teacher is required to provide learning situations
which will meet the objectives of that curriculum, the guidelines for
which are provided in detail by the State. If the common core curriculum
proposed by the English Inspectorate were to be imposed, it would to a
lesser extent be received. It would allow a broader interpretation of both
subject and syllabus.[4] However, learning situations in primary schools have
been greatly influenced by the ideas of Froebel and Piaget, and are pupil or
child-centred. At second level the public examinations in many countries
provide a received curriculum. However, as extract (3) above illustrates, in
many classrooms students are for the most part passive recipients of
knowledge. In this type of classroom there is a need for control. But these
are not the only kinds of teaching situation which can be used: role-playing
can be used in teaching modern languages, for example. The informal
learning will differ in these two circumstances,[5] and the disciplinary
requirements will also be different. The attitudes in the classroom where a
teacher negotiates the curriculum with the pupils will also be different, as
the writer of extract (4) above suggests.

There are no necessary correlations between teaching styles and the
curriculum. A highly structured class may be disciplined and happy
equally. A child-centred class may be undisciplined and unhappy. But what
is common to all situations is the influence of the teacher's perception of
his role: as the writer of extract (5) argues, this perception will 'determine
not just the aims of discipline but the aims of education for him'.

That changes in role perception can have a beneficial effect on teaching
could not be better exemplified than in part of the answer to the first
question by a student teacher of Irish, who wrote:

> I taught Irish history to 13 11-12-year-old boys. I wanted to teach them
> about the great social movements that make history. I wanted them to
> look beyond the facts and see why they happened and to ask
> themselves what movements or conflicts led to the physical
> manifestation? This was not what they learned. I was not long teaching
> my movements when I realized the class were desperately trying to
> relate it to the society they knew. This was what the class learned,
> ie that history is simply the story of how we live today. To be more
> precise what I really did was prepare them to think this way as they
> matured and other aspects of our society became clearer to them.
> What this meant for me was a reassessment of my view of society and
> our relationship with the pupils. My role changed. I became the
> chairman of a discussion group. My job was to make sure that those
> who had opinions aired them in a precise and lucid manner and to set
> the topic for the next discussion. My original idea of discipline had
> been a quiet class industriously taking notes. My classes were seldom

very quiet and we put the notes/conclusions we reached upon the blackboard and asked ourselves whether they were fair comments on our society. The fact that my perception of my role as teacher changed meant that the discipline brought about by our inter-actions changed both in its aims and manifestations. We imposed order because otherwise we could not have had a rational discussion and given every opinion an airing. We did not impose quietness so as I could lecture. We used a textbook and the class did homework because it gave a background and basis for questions and discussions; not because it was on the course. We did not complete the course but we discussed world history as well as Irish history, so that perhaps in some ways my original aim came close to fulfillment.

2.3 Teacher personality and performance

1. The teacher who is shy, unsure of himself will set himself aims of discipline which often resemble that of an army camp, so as to keep it quite clear as to who is boss. Nothing ever gets out of hand in any way. He asserts this aim by donning a gown or white coat, by standing at the top of the class and thus exerting dominance; 'a king ruling over his kingdom', an arrogant and perhaps not too successful method in its extremes.

2. Above all a teacher should use his charisma and resources power to avoid the dominant scene. I once saw a teacher in a class — he was very stern looking and by his appearance alone commanded authority. Yet he really did show empathy he had for them. He was a shy person himself and his stern outlook was really a facade. Though shy he did have a good sense of humour. On posing a question at which pupils sat looking terrified he waited a few moments and said, 'I can see you're alive — you twitch' — this broke all anxiety barriers — the pupils laughed and in the relaxed state they were able to pose solutions and discuss them. This teacher had the sense of the right moment — he was sensitive to them and could pick the appropriate thing to do at the right time.

3. Moving then from the question of professional competence to that of personality, it would seem that the teacher's approach to her class in general terms can be very influential in the atmosphere of the classroom. A teacher who accepts the pupils as individuals, and respects their separateness and privacy, has more chance of creating an atmosphere of trust. But this is not something that a teacher can decide at night that she will do with the class the next day. It comes from personality that has been formed through many experiences, inter-actions, and decisions in the past, and the continuing process of inter-action in the classroom will have its effect on the teacher. A teacher who has difficulties with an integrative approach (and it involves more short term risk for the teacher than a dominant role)

may well be tempted to revert to an authoritarian approach. There are many pressures in this direction. An integrative approach that goes wrong can create a noisy classroom and complaints from colleagues. An authoritarian approach can create the illusion of much work being done, and perhaps, in fact, the reality of work of a particular type. An authoritarian approach requires the teacher to give less of herself to the pupils and is less demanding on her professional skills.

These three responses show that the issue of personality in relation to discipline is complex. Shy people, as is evident from the second example, will not always behave in the same way as the person in the first. The authoritarian personality will be able to provide a happy and controlled learning system, but in a different way from the person whose orientation is democratic. To achieve such goals teachers need to have arrived at an understanding of their own role in this respect as well as a detailed understanding of both the way in which pupils learn and their own personality tendencies. Let us, therefore, for a few paragraphs consider the pupil as a learner.

2.4 Student learning and discipline

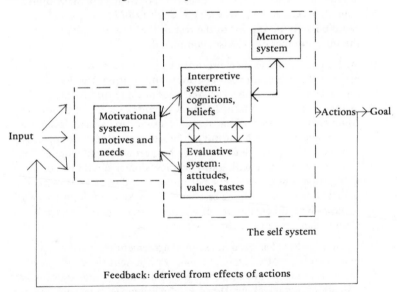

Figure 2.1 *A symbolic model of the learner.* From *Educational Psychology*, 2nd edition, by Frederick J McDonald. © 1965 by Wadsworth Publishing Company, Inc. Reprinted by permission of Wadsworth Publishing Company, Belmont, California 94002.

In the model shown in Figure 2.1 it is assumed that learning is a goal directed process. In the 'drive' to achieve the goal there are four response systems at work in the learner. There is a motivational system which will be discussed in great detail in Chapter 3, and which has a major influence over the direction of learning. Closely related to this system is an attitudinal system which makes judgements about the usefulness and value of the information which he is selecting, and related to these is the cognitive system which enables the learner to examine, frame, analyse and subsequently solve problems. Binding these together is a self-system which tells an individual about his effectiveness as a learner.

Inspection of some of the responses to the question about Mr X on p 21 illustrates the complexity of these inter-acting systems and the effect of teacher and school attitudes to the learner's disposition:

1. The class may be looked upon as another 'D stream' which has no chance of achieving anything. This may be the attitude of the school or even Mr X. To a large extent how pupils behave is conditioned by how they perceive people's perceptions of them, and the expectations which those people have for them. Such things probably explain the teacher's comments on Raymond's exercise and also no doubt have influenced Raymond's performance, eg 'Raymond — What difference does it make what I do, Mr X thinks I am no good anyway.' *This idea of a self-fulfilling prophecy*[6] could possibly be applied to the rest of the class and might explain the small number of exercises completed.

2. Mr X undermines his own authority by reverting to sarcasm which is never an advisable form of behaviour modification. His derisive reference to the boy's background does nothing for his (the boy's) or the teacher's self-image. Teachers should never revert to scathing comments and observations of pupils' homes and social class. Mr X does not seem to be in control of the situation. Checking copies at random is not a very definite act on his part and small wonder the boys try to get away with untidy copies. Copies should be collected at a certain time either at the beginning or end of class. If correction is to be done in school, the teacher must make an attempt to *see* all copies. The self-concept or self-image of these pupils is probably already damaged in a streamed situation.

3. Obviously there has been no 'school' agreement on disciplinary matters (or else Mr X ignored them). Having sent the child out of the class at lunch-time Mr X was taking a rather serious step for such a small matter as talking. However, the Principal, in my opinion, was wrong to have sent the child back in. Mr X may have been wrong to send him out initially but the Principal's action totally undermined Mr X's authority. The Principal should not have interfered but should have talked to Mr X about the situation afterwards.

4. Here, I might include a personal note: I found with weaker students
   — 50 per cent of my class — that such an encounter about
   homework be it positive or negative is best done outside class time.
   It is well known that the attention span of D stream pupils is weak
   and short lived and therefore in my opinion such diversions cannot
   be included during class time but are almost as important as giving
   a lesson.

Clearly these student teachers feel that the situation should not have
arisen. It is a sad fact of life that circumstances such as these are often
reported by student teachers. There *are* things which the teacher can do to
create an environment for learning: these respondents evidently think so,
as the illustrations in the next section show.

2.5 Creating an environment for learning in the classroom

(i) *Illustrating the importance of preparation and organization*

The teacher who organizes his classroom activities in a well-ordered
manner will see his role about discipline in a different light from the
teacher who is careless in his preparation. I found in Primary and
Secondary that when my lessons were well planned in advance, with
clear aims, objectives and goals, I had very few problems as regards
discipline. Not being sure of where I was going tended to create
problems of discipline. It is important too that children be involved
in the lesson and are not treated as passive elements which are there to
'soak up' knowledge. Passive children tended to be restless after a short
time whereas when they were involved in classroom activities they were
keen and interested in what they were doing.

(ii) *Illustrating the idea of a contract with the class relating to behaviour and the maintenance of a satisfactory physical environment*

Many of our student teachers have testified that they have found this
approach to be of considerable value.

A teacher will see his role in relation to discipline in a different manner
when he draws up a contract of rules with the class at the beginning of
the school year. No longer are children conforming to an unseen
authority which created rules. Their rules for classroom behaviour are
seen as having come from themselves. Infringement of class rules is an
infringement of what they themselves have set. In a way this leads to
the self-discipline I mentioned above.

I think that this aspect is very important because unless the teacher
brings about a growth in the pupil he is child-minding not teaching. By
helping him to make out rules of behaviour the pupils are taking

responsibility and this is an important role for them as *adolescents.*

(iii) Ripple and restitution: problems of implementation

To effect positive teacher-pupil relationships with regard to the aims of discipline, the teacher should try to be an 'unbiased practitioner', yet he/she must demonstrate to the class that he/she is fair. If favouritism towards one pupil is exhibited naturally discipline problems will arise. Objective deterrents towards unfavourable activities in the class may be achieved by the 'restitution' and 'ripple' effects. The restitution[7] effect is where the unfavourable stimulus is substituted by one more positive; this may be encouraged or achieved by the withdrawal of a positive reinforcer (reward),[8] until such time as the necessary discipline is acquired. The ripple effect,[9] as its name might suggest, is where the teacher makes an example of one child in order that the class may learn from it. (Author's note: this child may be chosen because of the high prestige he/she has among his/her peers in the class.) Whether this is actually effective in the long term is questionable. Certainly the teacher should consider the situation carefully, eg the sensitivity of the child, before utilizing the ripple effect.

(iv) Coping with minor misbehaviour

All teachers are advised by well documented studies to avoid confrontation of a direct nature; secondly to avoid raising the voice; thirdly to aim at silent gesture of staring hard at the offender or raising eyebrows.

If the teacher sees himself as the rigid disciplinarian he may in fact be encouraging misbehaviour in the classroom. If misbehaviour does occur the teacher should react in a cool passive manner without disrupting the whole class. Methods for coping effectively are:

1. approach the student but say nothing.
2. eye to eye contact.
3. a tap on the head or shoulder.
4. question such as 'John are you doing that problem I set you?'
5. statement 'You're not being fair to the rest of the class are you?'

2.6 Towards a learning environment

The examples I have chosen are not necessarily the best, and have tended to detract from more detailed discussion of the purposes and forms of punishment. Most textbooks suggest that wherever possible punishment should be a reinforcement to learning. In consequence the following should be avoided:

1. use of schoolwork as a punishment;

2. punishment which would cause mental stress;
3. physical sanctions.

I have always found there is a clear relation between student reading of the textbooks and implementation of discipline in their classes. Our student teachers have taken the advice of Good and Brophy (1973) that punishment should be used only when misbehaviour is repeated, not for single incidents of minor misbehaviour. All our students emphasize the need to treat all their pupils similarly in respect of both reward and punishment. Moreover the pupils must understand clearly the reasons for a rebuke or punishment.

Our students have also found the idea of behaviour modification useful. This concept uses the notions of reward and reinforcement to influence the development of good behaviour.

Finally mention should be made of the need for adequate school support. One of the respondents wrote:

> Teachers do not, however, work in isolation but within the structural framework of a school which may determine to some extent their perception of their role and consequent methods of discipline. For example, the teacher who firmly believes that he is the sole knowledge giver in the class and believes that disciplinary methods should have corporal punishment at the top of the list of effective means of controlling classroom behaviour, may have to modify such a perception if corporal punishment is forbidden by the school. On the other hand, the teacher who views himself as a guide and who encourages the children to discover for themselves and is tolerant of high noise levels may find himself restricted because of the general policy in the school of silent classes. Mostly, however, teachers adapt the available disciplinary methods to their particular perceptions of their role as teachers.

To quote Cohen and Mannion (1977): 'Your control of pupil behaviour will therefore be through a subtle blending of personal *power* emanating from your personality and skills and *authority* deriving from status and the established system of rules operating in the classroom.'

Much of what has been said above is contained in Hargreaves' (1972) summary of research findings on pupil attitudes to teachers. Broadly speaking, these suggest that pupils like teachers who keep good control, are fair, have no favourites, and give no extreme or immoderate punishments. One of my children has recently been subjected to lines which were given to the whole class because of the misbehaviour of a few. This is much resented, and is also a waste of time. Another of my children, when he was a prefect, set exercises which were relevant to the children's learning. He claims to have learned much by this approach, and it is certainly to be preferred. Children want discipline in order to learn. If they try, and if they sit in the front row and cannot hear because of other children's misbehaviour, they will resent both their classmates and the teacher. At the same time teachers must neither be too lax nor too strict. They must not pick on certain students. They must not threaten and then fail to carry out the threat: if they do this often, they will lose face and no notice will be taken of them.

If children cannot follow what is being said they are 'ready' to misbehave: lack of understanding is often a cause of irritability. As Bernstein has shown, there can be a communication gulf between teachers who use elaborated codes of language and children who use restricted codes which may extend to the misunderstanding of behaviour.[10] Many teachers go at too fast a pace and fail to explain concepts (see Chapter 6). This is especially true of mathematics: for the majority of pupils it is a difficult subject, and needs, as does any subject, to be made interesting. Pupils need help and the lesson needs to be paced so that help can be given. Children appreciate the teacher who 'knows his subject' and is well prepared: they know they will receive adequate help from such a person.

At the same time they do not like teachers who nag and ridicule them, or are tetchy and bad-tempered: what had happened at the teacher's breakfast table or during the drive to school should not influence his attitudes to the pupils. Children want their teacher to be friendly and understanding and to recognize them as individuals, different from one another, and with their own personal characteristics. This is not to say that teachers should not pull the legs of children in a good-humoured way: it is vindictiveness that should be avoided.

Regrettably, as some of the examples show, some teachers are influenced by such things as home background and modify their pupil appraisals accordingly. A recent investigation in a Canadian high school showed that appraisals of classroom behaviour were influenced by teacher perceptions of student life styles: students who had high psychoticism[11] scores on a personality inventory received a negative teacher appraisal; these students drank more alcohol, smoked more tobacco and marijuana, and tended to be male rather than female (Hurlburt, 1981).

In summary, as one of our students wrote in response to question (2) on p 21:

'Pupils respond well to considerate and positive treatment from adults' (Plowden Report). This, I think, is the key to the problem between Mr X and his class. The boys are D stream pupils. I have taught D to F stream pupils and found that criticism on my part was usually received by the class as being negative, and they resented it. A little bit of encouragement or careful wording so that all forms of criticism appeared as positive comments, eg 'Really! You are much cleverer than you appear to be from this exercise! Will you try harder next time and we'll see how you get on?' worked wonders. I think Mr X might do well to try it as it indicates that (a) the teacher feels positively about the child's ability; (b) he respects the child, and (c) he is treating him as a person in that he suggests that when the child makes the effort, both of them will work together on it.

Notes

1. Notional/functional syllabuses are discussed in Brumfit and Johnston (1979).

2. Kohlberg (1966) has described a theory of moral development which is non-relativistic; that is, all persons advance through stages of moral development, just as in Piaget's theory (Chapter 5) they advance through stages of intellectual development. These stages are not age-related and not every individual develops through all of them. Some never progress beyond the conventional level.

   A simplified version of these stages is shown in Exhibit 2.1.

---

1. *Stage 0.* Premoral stage

2. **Preconventional level**
   Stage 1. The punishment and obedience orientation
   Stage 2. The instrumental relativist orientation (right action consists of that which instrumentally satisfies one's own needs and occasionally the needs of others)

3. **Conventional level**
   Stage 3. Interpersonal concordance (good behaviour is that which pleases or helps others and is approved by them)
   Stage 4. Law and order orientation (right behaviour consists of doing one's duty, showing respect for authority and maintaining the given social order for its own sake)

4. **Postconventional, autonomous, or principled level**
   Stage 5. Social contract legalistic orientation (right action tends to be defined in terms of general individual rights and in terms of standards which have been critically examined and agreed upon by the whole society)
   Stage 6. The universal ethical principle orientation (right is defined by the decision of conscience in accord with self-chosen ethical principles appealing to logical comprehensiveness, universality and consistency). At this level there is a clear effort to define moral values and principles which have validity and application apart from the authority of the groups of persons holding these principles and apart from the individual's own identification with these groups

---

Exhibit 2.1 *Kohlberg's stages of moral development simplified.*
(As reproduced in Heywood (1977) with the permission of L Kohlberg.)

I have argued elsewhere that one of the difficulties which leads to an impedance in communication, as for example in industrial relations negotiations, might be that those concerned in such negotiations are at different levels of moral development. They would if Kohlberg is correct 'necessarily' have different views of what is 'right' in that context. This would make it exceptionally difficult for them to see one another's point of view, particularly if there were also language code difficulties.

3. *Some curriculum perspectives*

   (a) *Received perspective:* Curriculum knowledge is received and accepted as given. It is non-negotiable, non-dialectic and co-sensual. The new primary curriculum for national (primary) schools in Ireland which is prescribed by the State and controlled by the Inspectorate is a received curriculum.

   (b) *Reflexive perspective:* Curriculum knowledge is negotiable: content may be criticized and new curricula devised. Moreover, negotations may be undertaken with the pupils. The curriculum is dialectic and subject to many influences.

A public examination which allows schools to devise their own syllabuses and methods of assessment is reflexive in so far as individual subjects are concerned. However, the high status attached to some subjects means that the curriculum as a whole will be received.

(c) *Restructuring perspective:* Relates both the received and reflexive perspectives as two related modes of understanding both the realities of knowledge in the school curriculum and the possibilities of change therein. A public examination which allows a project to be determined by the pupil and marked by the teacher combines both perspectives.

Sociologists use these perspectives to examine how the curriculum can help the majority of students to enhance their expectations of power and their capacity to exercise it, as well as how it can play a part in bringing about a social situation in which these expectations and capacities can be used.

The sociology of the curriculum is discussed in Eggleston (1977). See also Chapter 8, section 7.

4. The Irish curriculum is in the two volumes of *Primary School Curriculum* (1971), Dublin: Department of Education. For ideas relating to the common core curriculum see *Curriculum 11-16 (1977)*, Working Papers by HM Inspectorate, London: Department of Education and Science.

5. A large amount of informal learning takes place in schools independently of the formal curriculum. This informal or *hidden* curriculum is essential if the pupils are to survive. It stems from the need to learn forms of behaviour which are acceptable to both their peers and their teachers. In some circumstances, the peer group may disapprove of high grades, and in this case an able person might be induced to perform at a level lower than he is able. In some circumstances cheating may be given tacit approval. A similar behaviour pattern was found among work groups in the famous Hawthorne studies in the Westinghouse Company in Chicago, which led to the idea of formal and informal organization in industry. Eggleston (1977) gives a particularly good example when he suggests that it can be argued that the purpose of mathematics teaching is not only to help pupils learn mathematics but also to allow some of them to realize that they cannot learn mathematics (see also note 6 below).

6. *Self-fulfilling prophecy*

Teachers who expect certain students to behave intelligently and others to behave poorly may communicate that expectation in such a way that the students behave in this way. This has also been called the *Pygmalion effect*. Teachers may believe things about a child which are not true: the belief is conveyed to the child in some way, who then behaves in the manner expected.

Good and Brophy (1973) put it this way:

(1) Specific behaviours and achievements are expected from particular children.

(2) In consequence of these expectations the teacher behaves in different ways towards each child.

(3) When a teacher tells a child about the behaviour and achievements expected of it (as in the examination question which opened this chapter), the child's self-concept, motivations and aspirations are affected.

(4) If there is no resistance to consistent treatment of the same kind the child will tend to shape his achievements and behaviours with those beliefs (see note 5 above), and in time achievements and behaviour conform more and more with what is expected of him.

7. *Restitution effect:* Reparation for an injury (misbehaviour) when related to discipline.

8. *Reinforcement:* The strengthening of something which is learned, for example by repetition immediately or some days afterwards. A reinforcer is an event which strengthens behaviour. If a person is offered a reward on several occasions for the same behaviour it will influence learning in that direction.

9. *Ripple effect:* Effect on a class of pupils of a command to and response from one pupil. Some authorities suggest that the pupil has to have high prestige within the group. Negative as well as positive ripples can be created.

10. Bernstein (1961) distinguished between a *restricted code* of language used by those in lower socioeconomic status groups and an *elaborated code* used by those in higher economic status groups. The restricted code limits both scope of expression and thought. It progressively orients the child to a lower level of conceptualization. It is the language of implicit meaning in which it becomes difficult to make explicit, and to elaborate verbally, subjective intent.

    The teacher who speaks with an elaborated code has, according to Bernstein, to make available that code without depriving the pupil of the dignity of his own restricted code. Some characteristics of the restricted code are:

    □ short, grammatically simple, often unfinished sentences
    □ simple and repetitive use of conjunctions
    □ little or no use of subordinate clauses
    □ rigid and limited use of adjectives and adverbs
    □ frequent use of statements where the reason and conclusion are confounded to produce a categoric statement.

11. It is found when the Eysenck personality inventory is used that high psychoticism scorers are solitary, do not care for people, are often cruel and inhumane, lack feeling and empathy, and are insensitive (Eysenck and Eysenck, 1975). The Canadian investigation is described in Hurlburt (1981).

References

B Bernstein (1961) Social structure, language and learning, *Educational Research*, 3, 163-76.

C J Brumfit and K Johnston (eds) (1979) *The Communicative Approach to Language Teaching*. Oxford: Oxford University Press.

L Cohen and L Mannion (1977) *A Guide to Teaching Practice*. London: Methuen.

J Eggleston (1977) *The Sociology of the School Curriculum*. London: Routledge and Kegan Paul.

H J Eysenck and S B G Eysenck (1975) *Edits Manual of the EPQ*. San Diego, Cal: Educational and Industrial Testing Service.

T L Good and J E Brophy (1973) *Looking in Classrooms*. New York: Harper and Row.

D Hargreaves (1972) *Interpersonal Relations and Education*. London: Routledge and Kegan Paul.

J Heywood (1977) *Assessment in Higher Education*. London: Wiley.

G Hurlburt (1981) Psychoticism, teacher appraisal and life styles of a Canadian high school sample, *Alberta Journal of Educational Research*, 28 (3), 211-16.

L Kohlberg (1966) Moral education in schools: a developmental view, *School Review*, 74, 1-30.

3 Motivation

3.1 Questions which have been asked on motivation in teacher training examinations

1. Distinguish between *extrinsic* and *intrinsic* motivation. What do you do to improve intrinsic motivation in the subjects you teach?
2. Discuss the relationships between arousal, anxiety, frustration and IQ. Describe any experiment you know which supports your conclusions.
3. Distinguish between motives, needs, arousal, drive and expectancy. Illustrate your answer by reference to one theory of human motivation.
4. 'Motivation is a necessary but not sufficient condition of learning.' Discuss this statement in relation to the performance of high and low anxiety students.
5. 'Teachers should aim to remove all tension from pupils if learning is to be optimized.' Discuss with reference to recently reported research on this topic.
6. 'The complexity of human motivation is evident when we think of persistent motivational dispositions which differ from one man to another. These dispositions may be quiescent or become manifest in behaviour under conditions of appropriate motivational arousal' (Hilgard, 1971). What are the major factors which govern 'conditions of appropriate motivational arousal?'
7. 'Some anxiety is necessary in learning.' Discuss, illustrating your answer by reference to reported research and your experience in initial training.
8. An applicant for next year's Higher Diploma course (second level initial training) asks you about the relevance of educational research in the area of motivation. What would you tell him? Take into account its validation by your own experience in the classroom.

The examples in the sections which follow are taken from answers to question 8.

PART I: MOTIVATION, NEEDS AND BEHAVIOUR

3.2 Motivation, discipline and method

In my own class I had a problem with one boy who was very quiet but constantly prodding the boys in front who would tell me and I reacted by reprimanding him. He would react by talking to me about something totally different. My supervisor suggested that he needed more attention. She pointed out that I was not consistent in paying attention to him. I would for a while then totally withdraw it till he annoyed a pupil again. I found it hard to believe that a pupil could be more satisfied with reprimands than being ignored, but I paid much more attention to him and amazingly the prodding stopped and he began offering to answer questions and his work improved. What I also discovered by chance was that he was a very gifted artist and so he is able to do visual aids for me which has motivated him very much.

Inevitably, as one of the respondents to the question on discipline wrote, all learning must begin with motivation. Like many other authors, he did not attempt to define motivation, but assumed that the assessor would understand what he meant. However, he did say that it was the energy source on which higher structures of knowledge would be built, and his overall point was that motivation in language classes would be achieved by a variety of methods, which would inevitably help discipline.

Another student referred to work by Clarizio (1971) when she described a comprehensive plan of motivation and discipline. Clarizio suggests a contract with the class, and this student teacher made the pupils draw up a list of rewards as well as the work elements in the contract. Effective performance could mean that homework was *not* given, or if the work was completed ahead of schedule magazines could be looked at. A pupil of the week read out the weekly vocabulary test and did not participate in it. The pupils, this student reports, liked this approach which is similar to that used by many primary school teachers.

As one student respondent said:

The use of incentives can be amazing. I thought on entering teaching that praise and encouragement would not be effective, particularly to the older age set. However, I now use it to all age groups, with effect. This incentive does not only come in verbal form. Marking of copies and such like can also be an incentive. Incentives from within come from the solution of problems, and completion of previously hard problems.

The use of punishment is something I seek to avoid. Punishment can take many forms, and usually amounts to no more than the withdrawal of incentives. Nevertheless, the use of punishment has a place in the area of motivation. As something which the students seek to avoid, it can be a powerful tool in the hands of the teacher.

3.3 Needs, discipline and learning

By looking at the needs of individual pupils one can learn a lot about a class. In my own teaching I noticed one boy who never made an effort to work or to listen and could be bold in class. I never heard him speak until we started to study plant structures. This was something he knew and so I allowed him to draw diagrams on the board and to explain it to the class. I soon found out that his need was to succeed. His work began to improve, he felt he was succeeding and now continues to achieve. What he needed was a taste of success.

Clearly there is a relationship between discipline and motivation. This will be better understood, as the examples in Chapter 2 show, if we understand the 'needs' of individuals, for *motives* arise out of 'needs', which are relatively permanent tendencies in individuals to be motivated in specific directions (ways). H A Murray (1938) has defined 'needs' as psychological forces that organize action and other cognitive processes toward its own satisfaction.

There are many classifications of 'needs'. It seems generally agreed that in an individual there are:

1. a set of basic 'needs';
2. 'needs' which have been acquired in the culture in which he finds himself,

and that the need system of an individual depends on his state of development.

Maslow (1943) makes a useful distinction between primary and secondary needs. The primary ones are basic, such as the needs for water, food, sex, lactation, urination, defecation, heat avoidance and cold avoidance. The secondary needs vary from person to person. We would say that their profile represents a particularized picture of an individual's personality. Seen as needs, or social motives, these words become valuable tools for the teacher. Murray's list of social motives is as follows:

abasement	to surrender, accept punishment, confess, atone; to depreciate oneself
achievement	to overcome obstacles; to strive to do something difficult
acquisition	to work for, gain possessions; to grasp
affiliation	to form friendships and associations
aggression	to assault or injure; to belittle, harm, blame, accuse
autonomy	to resist influence or coercion; to strive for independence
blamavoidance	to be well behaved and obey the law; to avoid blame
cognizance	to explore, to satisfy curiosity
construction	to organize and build
counteraction	to refuse defeat by restriving or retaliation
defendance	to defend oneself against blame or belittlement; to justify oneself
deference	to serve gladly; to admire and follow
dominance	to influence or control others
exhibition	to attract attention to one's person
exposition	to point and demonstrate; to relate facts

harmavoidance	to avoid pain; to take precautionary measures
infavoidance	to avoid failure, shame, humiliation
nurturance	to nourish, aid or protect the helpless
order	to arrange, order, put away objects
play	to relax, amuse oneself
rejection	to snub, ignore, or exclude
retention	to retain possession of things; to refuse to give or lend
sentience	to seek and enjoy sensuous impressions
sex	to form and further an erotic relationship; to have sexual intercourse
succorance	to seek aid, protection or sympathy
superiority	to achieve and be recognized for one's achievement
understanding	to abstract; to discriminate among concepts; to synthesize ideas

Freud was the first person to analyse the relationships between behaviour and needs. Most people would associate him with the view that neuroses are due to sex repression. J Powell associates him with the pleasure principle. Within each of us, Freud suggested, there is a source of energy, which he called the *id*, and which is manifested in our emotional drives. It is a basic drive for pleasure: the term *libido* (the Latin for desire or lust) is used by Freud to describe the instinctual energies which derive from the *id*. Within each person, there is a *superego* which moderates this basic desire for pleasure. There is thus in every person a continuing tension between wish and morality which is resolved by the *ego* (the self). The pleasure drive is the fundamental drive in human beings. Frustration of the libido is a basic cause of neuroses.

Adler thought differently. He argued that sex and the libido were to be seen in terms of the struggle by an individual to gain power, and that all relationships are to be interpreted as struggles for power. Powell (1978) associates him with the power principle of behaviour and contrasts this with the principle of avoidance of responsibility which is the fundamental of Skinner's behaviourism. Skinner argues that if a particular piece of behaviour is found rewarding we repeat it: if the behaviour produces a harmful result we avoid it and so on. This theory, which is called *operant conditioning*, is a theory of behavioural determinism. (The use of the term 'behavioural' here is very different from that of the term 'behavioural objective', which I use in my work on examinations; because Skinner uses the same phrase the two are confused. The reasons for this will be explained in Chapter 8.) Skinner's important contribution to educational method was undoubtedly the development of programmed learning.
learning.

Freud's theory of human development has been of particular import-ance to the study of child development. We now accept the importance of the first five or so years of a child's life and realize that the child has to be helped through those stages with great care. The ego-defence mechanisms which Freud highlighted are given below in a simplified form (after Coleman, 1950). They are mechanisms employed, to a greater or lesser extent, by us all, to make life more comfortable; only when over-used are they potentially harmful, sometimes causing illness. Obviously, it is useful for the teacher to know what these mechanisms are, since they clearly influence learning and learning difficulties.

Mechanism	Function
denial of reality	Protection of self from unpleasant reality by refusal to perceive it
fantasy	Gratification of frustrated desires in imaginary achievements
compensation	Offset of weaknesses by emphasis of desirable trait or recompense for frustration in one area by over-gratification in another
identification	Increase of feelings of worth by association with person or institution of illustrious standing
introjection	Incorporation of external values and standards into ego structure so the individual is not at their mercy as external threats
projection	Placement of blame for difficulties upon others or attribution of one's own unethical desires to others
rationalization	Attempt to prove that one's behaviour is 'rational' and justifiable and thus worthy of self and social approval
repression	Prevention of painful or dangerous thoughts from entering the consciousness
reaction formation	Prevention of dangerous desires from being expressed by exaggerating opposed attitudes and types of behaviour and using them as 'barriers'
displacement	Discharge of pent-up feelings, usually of hostility, on objects less dangerous than those which initially aroused the emotions
emotional insulation	Withdrawal into passivity to protect self from hurt
isolation	Isolation of affective charge from hurtful situations or separation of incompatible attitudes by logic-tight compartments
regression	Retreat to earlier developmental level involving less mature responses and usually a lower level of aspiration
sublimation	Gratification of frustrated sexual desires in substitute non-sexual activities
undoing	Atonement for and thus counteraction of immoral desires and acts

There is clearly a relationship between needs and behaviour. An investigation by Frenkel-Brunswick (1942) led to the following more detailed definitions:

Needs	
need for autonomy	Tendency to strive for independence and freedom; desire to be free from social ties, to shake off influence, coercion, and restraint; relatively little care for conventions and group ideology; tendency to act as one pleases
need for social ties, social acceptance	Desire to be generally well-liked; to conform to custom, to join groups, to live sociably, to be accepted by a group in any form, to make contacts

need for achievement	Desire to attain a high standard of objective accomplishment; to increase self-regard by successful exercise of talent, to select hard tasks; high aspiration level
need for recognition	Desire to excite praise and commendation, to demand respect, social approval, prestige, honours and fame
need for abasement	Tendency to self-depreciation, self-blame or belittlement; to submit passively to external forces, to accept injury, blame, criticism, punishment; tendency to become resigned to fate, to admit inferiority and defeat, to confess, to seek punishment and misfortune; masochistic tendency
need for aggression	Desire to deprive others, be belittling, attacking, ridiculing, depreciating
need for succorance	Desire for support from outside, from people, institutions, or supernatural agencies
need for control (dominance)	Desire to control one's human environment, by suggestion, by persuasion or command
need for escape	Tendency to escape all unpleasant situations — to avoid blame, hardship, etc; to project own failures on others or on circumstances; to gain immediate pleasure with inability to postpone pleasure; use of fantasy, etc

Behaviour can be described in the same way:

grooming	Spending a great deal of time in grooming self: frequently arranging or combing hair, brushing off clothes, putting on make-up
energetic	Overtly active almost all the time, including gross movements and aggressive contacts with physical environment; eager, animated, bodily movements
interested in opposite sex	Continually initiates contacts with and takes every opportunity to attract attention of members of opposite sex, for activities in which sexes are mixed
socially participative	Takes every opportunity for social contact allowed by the nature of the situation. Continually directs attention toward others, talks to them and participates in activities with them
seeking adult company	Seeks out adults in preference to children in a group. Hangs around adults making frequent bids for attention. Identifies self with adults. Very cordial to adults
resistant to authority	Deliberately breaks rules. Refuses to comply with requests of person in charge. Subtly resists authority; evasive, sly, two-faced, smooth, in contrast to: eager to comply with adults' wishes; anticipates what adults must want; asks adult assistance in enforcing regulations; extremely suggestible with adults
socially self-confident	Very assured behaviour with both adults and children. Takes failure in matter-of-fact way. Invites new situations requiring poise and confidence
attention-seeking	Constantly seeks to put self in a conspicuous position, bluffing, showing off. Makes strenuous efforts to gain recognition of associates
sensitive and dependent	Excessively concerned about the sort of impression he makes on his associates. Very sensitive and easily 'hurt'. Reacts strongly to praise or blame. Constantly leaning on others for approval of his actions, or help in decisions

> *seeking* Highly successful in influencing the group either directly
> *leadership* or by indirect suggestion. Competent in organizing and
> handling group activities. Comments or suggestions
> welcomed by the group and readily accepted

It may be argued that these definitions are commonly understood. But even if we are aware of these definitions, are we likely to make use of them as teachers? It seems unlikely, unless we consider them seriously. Let me reinforce this from a view of a factory at work. Exhibit 3.1 shows what a training officer (W Humble) saw on a one-day tour round his factory. Should its management have been pleased? Suppose you found the same thing happening in your classroom. Could you predict similar kinds of behaviour among the pupils in your class?

I. *Reaction to suggestions between workers and their managers*
  (1) 'It won't work.'
  (2) 'We've tried all that before.'
  (3) 'I have bigger problems than that.'
  (4) 'I'll think about it, when I have more time.'
  (5) 'Do you want me to do your job as well as my own?'
  (6) 'What do you think I pay you for.'

II. *Confrontations between workers and their managers*
  (1) 'What's in this for us.'
  (2) 'You've had your say — let us have ours.'
  (3) 'That's typical management thinking.'
  (4) 'That's not for me to decide, but the members will.'
  (5) 'It's not my idea — it's the boss's.'
  (6) 'Let the folk above make the decision.'
  (7) 'Don't ask me — I'm just the message boy.'
  (8) 'OK the man who pays the piper calls the tune.'
  (9) 'Not my job.'
  (10) 'You're the manager.'
  (11) 'See me about that later.'
  (12) 'Who do you think you are?'

III. *Expressions of indifference while at work and in front of managers*
  (1) Making phone calls.
  (2) Tidying up desk.
  (3) Writing (eg signing of letters).
  (4) Looking through papers while answering in monosyllables.
  (5) Combing hair.
  (6) Manicuring finger nails.
  (7) Refilling cigarette lighter.

IV. *Expressions of impatience*
  (1) Yawning.
  (2) Looking at the time.
  (3) Tapping on the desk.
  (4) Answering in monosyllables.
  (5) Tone of voice.

Exhibit 3.1 *Behaviour at work: some observations by training officers. (Given to the author by W Humble, a training officer in industry.)*

The real problem for student teachers is that they are not trained in such analysis of needs and behaviour, as this example from a student response shows. It is given as a warning without comment on the accuracy of its judgement.

A warning in regard to needs in association with motivation must be given. Needs cannot be inferred directly from behaviour as obsessional behaviour does not necessarily equate with the need. Again an actual situation shows this clearly. A student of lower ability than the rest of the class tended to do little homework, if any. However, I knew her home situation was unstable and so excused her (she also tends to be absent regularly). I thought it would help her to get individual attention from the teacher for remedial maths students. It transpired that her need was to have continued individualized attention: if it was given to her, her level of aspiration and motivation rose. However, the needs which I had inferred were different. I would definitely say that current research in motivation has helped me.

Another wrote in response to a question on discipline:

A lot of research in industry, particularly regarding motivation, is claimed to be relevant also in the classroom situation. Regarding people's attitudes to work two theories have arisen. Theory X believes that people in general do not like work and will avoid it where possible; the implications for managers (and teachers) are that they must continuously push and threaten. Theory X has been recently replaced by theory Y. This theory believes that people in general like to work and would welcome some responsibility. Both of the above theories allow for some individuals who are an exception to the general rule.

There is also another view about the relationship between needs, drives and learning, developed by Abraham Maslow. Maslow believes that needs are hierarchically ordered, and that we are all trying to reach the top of the hierarchy or ladder (see Figure 3.1). The highest state of independence and excellence he calls self-actualization. Not everyone reaches this level, and according to Maslow we are at our best when we are striving for something which we do not possess. One of the student teachers described her role as helping the child to 'learn for its own sake', a much hackneyed phrase which gains considerably when it is placed in the context of self-actualization.

Theory Y is in many respects based on the concept of self-actualizing man. If we look at all these different models we find, as Daniel and McIntosh (1972) found when they analysed industrial research, that there is no simple answer. They wrote:

In terms of understanding workers' [students'] behaviour and attitudes, the critical question is often not the one so frequently posed of *what* are people [students] really interested, or most interested in, or *whether* they are more interested in job [study] satisfaction and intrinsic rewards, but rather *when* are they interested in intrinsic rewards and *when* are they interested in extrinsic rewards?

The position in respect of students would seem to be the same, as my substitutions in the brackets illustrate.

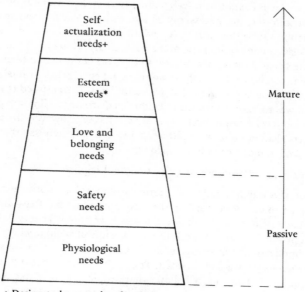

+ Desires to know and understand
* Desires for achievement recognition

Figure 3.1 *Self-actualizing man* (after Maslow, 1943)

C F Carter in his Presidential Address to the Society for Research into Higher Education (1972), said:

> I have three children, all of whom appear to have high achievement motivation. I will not risk embarrassing them by going into details, but I note that the nature of the motivation is quite different in each case — it is therefore summoned forth by different sets of circumstances, and their methods of work are very different. I suspect, therefore, that the difficulty which we find in improving the motivation of our students arises from the unappreciated variety of our human material. The state of keen competition which will stimulate some to great efforts will drive others into hopelessness and apathy. The things which induce some, repel others. One day we shall learn that it is necessary to differentiate our teaching and examining methods more than we do at present, so as to make them appropriate to the characteristics of the very different types of student who come to us.

In these circumstances, is it possible to have a satisfactory model of the learner and, if it is, what are its implications for assessment, teaching and learning? Once again, a parallel is to be found in the studies of organization and management theory. Man, argues Schein (1965), is complex and likely to 'differ from his neighbour in the patterns of his complexity'. Inevitably learners are no different, for man and learner are the same thing and learning is essential to motivation, be it at work or in college. A picture of the complex learner emerges thus:

1. The learner is complex. He is highly variable. He has many motives, some of which are more important than others. The order of importance is likely to change from time to time with changing circumstances. Since his motive patterns are complex, his response to incentives will also change with circumstances.

2. The learner is capable of learning new motives through his curriculum and institutional experiences. The psychological contract he makes with his teachers and the institution is the result of a complex interaction between perceived needs and learning and institutional experiences.

3. The learner's motives in different institutions or different subsystems of the same institution may be different; the student who is alienated in the formal structure may find fulfillment of his social and self-actualization needs in the student union or other parts of the extra-mural system or outside the system altogether. If the curriculum structure is complex in respect of perceived needs or apparent abilities, some parts of the curriculum may engage some motives while other parts engage other motives.

4. The learner can become productively involved with the curriculum and institution on the basis of many different kinds of motive. His ultimate satisfaction in the institution depends only in part on the nature of his motivation. The nature of the task to be performed, the abilities and experience of the learner and the nature of teachers and administrators in the institution all interact to produce a certain pattern of work and feelings.

5. The learner can respond to many different kinds of learning strategy depending on his own motives and abilities and the nature of the task. There is no one correct learning strategy which will work for all learners at all times.

A whole area of study has been devoted to the understanding of children, but it is beyond the scope of this chapter. Nevertheless, some questions on this topic are given below, in the hope that they will stimulate study and observation and provide a little advanced organization for the student not only in initial training but in the years which follow when experience is being consolidated.

1. In what ways do the needs which children have influence their behaviour? Illustrate with examples from your own experience,

avoiding examples which relate to social class.

2. In what ways is tension in the classroom likely to influence ego-defensive action in the teacher and how might this affect learning in the class? Illustrate, if possible from your own experience.

3. Self-realization is one of Maslow's higher needs. To what extent is it in conflict with that tradition of education which aims to teach pupils to care for others?

PART II: MOTIVATION IN THE CLASSROOM

3.4 Advanced organizers moving from the general to the specific

1. Motivation, therefore, may be regarded as an energy change in a person which is associated with behaviour directed toward the attainment of a goal. It is an increase in the vigour of human activity. A person becomes energized to achieve a goal. On entering a class the teacher has to arouse (arousal function) to achieve the goals of that lesson. To do this she will have to create expectations (expectancy function) among the pupils. During the class the teacher will try to prevent frustration, through the use of incentives (incentive function) related to disciplinary procedures (disciplinary function).

2. In drawing up a class plan it is important to think of the motivation factors — work out what will arouse the class, what will make them interested in what you want them to learn. To many classes, Irish grammar may seem a boring topic — but if one can relate the verb 'to go' to their out-of-school activities, eg rugby — going to an international match, the names of the players who came over, who is going to play, the result of the match — the level of arousal and interest will be quite different from that of simply learning the verb rote fashion. The pupils will really want to learn it in order to express their ideas.

3. I never realized how important it is to vary the expectancy. A rather boring story in an Irish lesson can be made stimulating by role-playing, for example. Variety remains one of the most important aspects. I found this out the hard way. I had found a way to make a dull Irish class interesting: role-playing, the children asking questions themselves. After encouraging this participation for some time I suddenly discovered that they were tired of it and I had to return to the traditional style.

4. The entering characteristics of the pupil are also a source of motivation. The children must be at a level between boredom and frantic emotional activity in order to be motivated to learn. Thus the teacher must awaken the bored and passive, the overactive. I have found the most useful method of achieving this is by means of a

dramatic introduction.

This leads to a further point which the researcher tells us. The child must know what he is to do if he is to be motivated to do it. Thus I have found it most successful to say that we are going to do A, B, C today instead of ploughing into A without mentioning B and C. Knowing what is to be done in a class often encourages the pupil and means work can be covered more quickly.

5. It is not surprising that very few pupils have attempted the homework for as I have stated above Mr X does not seem to have an order or method as to correction nor does he seem to have had any real purpose in giving the homework. As regards homework, one must have a purpose — it can be used either as an incentive, or for assessing understanding or entering behaviour, or to give feedback to both pupil and teacher. Evaluation studies have shown this has a positive effect on learning and discipline for it is then obvious the teacher knows what he is doing and is trying to help the pupils.

Since we have already dealt with the disciplinary problem in the previous chapter this function of the teacher will not be dealt with any more. A separate section with its own organizers is included on the incentive function.

3.5 Entering characteristics: another model of the teaching process

It should be clear by now that the entering characteristics which a pupil has are of considerable importance to his performance in the class. These characteristics can be related to many factors, including intelligence, aptitude, interests, personality and, as so many examination answers indicate, social class. Even so, for any class of a given age there is likely to be a general band of intelligence and interest which, although wide, makes the pupils teachable. Mixed ability teaching does, however, require some training, and for this reason it is discussed later in this book (see Chapter 6).

The breadth of information which these characteristics contain is no better illustrated than by D E Murphy's Student Profile (see Appendix 1). This was developed as an instrument for school-based assessment. Its sophistication, which goes far beyond the judgements of teachers in the staffroom, arises from the need to make the instrument reliable if it is to have credibility (see Heywood, 1978).

These characteristics should not be confused with those pertaining to the motivation of pupils as they begin a class, although of course they are contributory. A quick look at the description of the hidden curriculum on p 34 will underline the significance of peer-group behaviour. So there are several categories of entering characteristics. Example 4 above (p 46) relates them to goals which necessarily requires a plan of campaign. Problems associated with the determination of objectives and the design of lesson plans are dealt with in Chapter 8. At this stage it will suffice to draw attention to the model of the instruction and evaluation process which must arise if all the different things which have been said about teaching and learning are now put together, as in Figure 3.2.

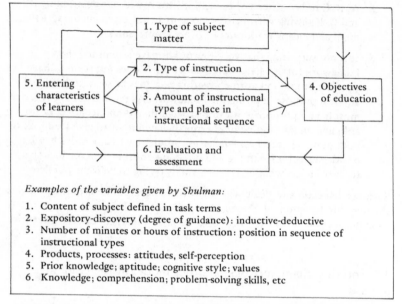

Examples of the variables given by Shulman:

1. Content of subject defined in task terms
2. Expository-discovery (degree of guidance): inductive-deductive
3. Number of minutes or hours of instruction: position in sequence of instructional types
4. Products, processes: attitudes, self-perception
5. Prior knowledge; aptitude; cognitive style; values
6. Knowledge; comprehension; problem-solving skills, etc

Figure 3.2 *Theoretical generalization about the nature of evaluation and instruction.* (Based on Shulman's (1970) generalization of Cronbach's view of the nature of instruction; modified by Heywood (1978) by the inclusion of Box 6.)

We can go one step further and arrive at a model of the teacher's decision-making process. Figure 3.3 shows it to relate inputs to outputs or goals. Stages 2, 3, 4 and 5 represent the operations we undertake in order to make a decision or reach a goal. Teaching goals are learning goals, so every decision which is made in the class is, to quote McDonald, a hypothesis about learning. Very often the wrong judgements are made and a new start has to be made. Nevertheless, as the last of the organizers to this section shows, learning has to be planned for. Decisions in the classroom and prior plans are hypotheses about the factors which will produce learning in the class. They take into account the entering characteristics and motivations of the students, hence the importance attached to lesson planning in this text (see Chapter 8).

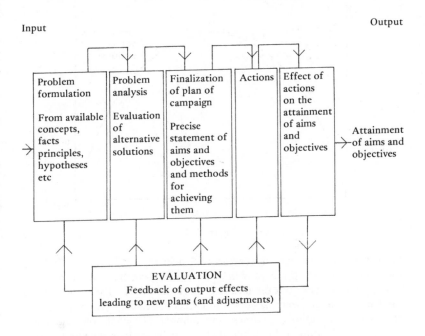

Input   Output

Attainment of aims and objectives

Figure 3.3 *A model of decision making (problem solving).* (See also Exhibit 7.1 and McDonald (1968: p 60) for an alternative model. The use of the term aims and objectives is related to Chapters 7 and 8. Goal is an equally acceptable alternative.)

3.6 Arousal and expectancy

Most students will happily draw a model of our state during one day, from deep sleep through waking to an optimal level of attention, and thence decline to sleep. It is likely to follow in most respects the diagram in Figure 3.4. Hebb (1955), who first drew attention to these changes, noted that our efficiency decreased because of interferences from our emotions, and thus anxiety.

In many respects our behaviour during lectures follows a similar pattern as does that of pupils in the classroom. Thus the teacher has an arousal function: the introductory phase of each lesson is concerned with motivation, that is, with arousal.

The teacher's task, put simply, is to prevent boredom on the one hand and too much stimulation on the other. Learning will not take place in a child when he is very excited. On the other hand it is unlikely to take place if the child is very bored. Tasks have to be set which relate to the abilities, drives and interests of the pupil. Unfortunately, the arousal states of pupils in a class are likely to be at several different levels. As will

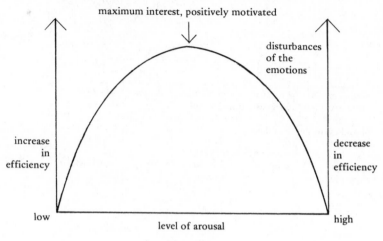

Figure 3.4

be seen in the section on incentives (3.7 below), some students find that their arousal level optimizes with some anxiety and frustration; this does not apply for others, but the idea that there should be no anxiety (tension) or frustration in learning does not seem tenable. Other pupils are stimulated by curiosity: witness the number of people old and young trying to do a 'rubic cube' while they are walking along the street. Others simply cannot face doing puzzles. The teacher is thus faced with the general problem of class arousal as well as with the specific problem of individual responses.

Expectancy, as used by de Cecco and Crawford (1974), is a momentary belief that a particular outcome will follow a particular act. In relation to classroom teaching, it is useful to think of the expectations which pupils have of what will happen in the class, as well as the ability of the teacher to create expectations within the class. But this is to lose the 'momentary' aspect of the definition.

The value of the 'momentary' is that it relates our instantaneous behaviour to what we see. If there is a discrepancy between what we see and what we expected to see, we may become angry. For instance, if we enter a classroom and find people jumping on the desks when we expected to see them sitting and reading, then there is a discrepancy between expectation and perception which causes anger. Such discrepancies are sources of arousal. It has been suggested that a small discrepancy will cause us to feel pleasant while a large discrepancy will cause unpleasant feelings.

Expectancy is also accompanied by estimates of the level of satisfaction which will be obtained. Psychologists call this valence. This is not the same as enjoying the outcome when we have it. The concept of valence explains some aspects of human behaviour. De Cecco illustrates this point with the example of under-achievers. A pupil who has the ability to achieve

50

academically has a high expectancy of success. If he does not get any satisfaction from academic success (low valence), he may not do as well as he could. Such pupils are called *under-achievers*: they are not motivated to achieve, nor do they expect to succeed. Even the prospect of failure will not produce a higher level of drive.

The teacher has thus to maintain the pupils in a state of willingness to learn. This he achieves with teaching strategies, which range from simple questioning to complex projects. He achieves the expectancy function by first defining what is expected of the pupils, and then modifying the pupils' expectations in such a way that they are encouraged to pursue the teacher's objectives. This activity is related to the incentive function, for pupils often value their achievements in terms of their success and failure; it is, as we shall see, a problem of personality.

3.7 Incentives (external and intrinsic motivation)

(a) The organizers

X has outlined his belief that a pupil's ability to experiment with his own surroundings and feel that he is the origin of his own behaviour rather than a simple pawn is very important. He also was one of the first to put forward his belief that extrinsic motivators may in fact lessen the motivation if intrinsic motivation is already present. Funnily enough I had experience of this situation several months before I had actually read this research. As a first task I had allowed the pupils to work in groups and produce dialogues in French to be dramatized before the class; on the second attempt I said that the test would win a small prize. To my surprise the content of the dialogues was not as good as the first lot. I had not thought about the reason for this but it could in fact have been due to making pupils feel more in power again by placing an extrinsic motivator on them.

A few pupils feel they have certain rights and that they can structure their learning in certain ways and choose certain learning goals.

If you want a pupil to perform well there are numerous incentives you can give apart from praise. My first years are writing novels and one boy who had the intrinsic motivation to write didn't actually get very far. In order to give him extrinsic motivation I offered him 5p a page for some work. It was done with relish and great interest but it will not stop there — he has more to do with the spur of intrinsic motivation.

Extrinsic motivation consists of awarding prizes, stars, praise, sweets, giving jobs, seats of honour, etc. It is good to use extrinsic motivation sparingly and usually, say, with kids who are not intrinsically motivated. I have one particular boy in my class who will do almost anything for a bar of chocolate, he is not intrinsically motivated, but if you produce a Yorkie bar his effort increases. To use the same motives with others would cause them to make less effort. Biehler says that children who enjoy doing certain things, if they are rewarded for them will like them less. So one must be very careful.

Success breeds success as failure breeds failure. Therefore, for the weaker ones it is necessary to minimize their failings, set goals within their reach (give them easier tasks). When they achieve something, make them feel it is because of their efforts. I have a very weak sixth year pupil who has no confidence in herself. One day, I was talking to her and she told me grammar was her problem — she could not understand any of it. Since then, I have gone through small sections — individual items — with her, step by step, and made her feel that after each one was achieved it was because of her effort — she has improved. If she fails, I make her believe it was lack of effort on her part, not an incapability to do the thing.

(b) Commentary

These organizers admirably show the incentive function of teachers and how incentives, including the self-fulfilling hypothesis, can be used with effect.

I must confess to some alarm when I read these extracts. During the war when I was in the first-year class of a secondary school the English master simply could not keep order. Bedlam reigned. But he made the matter worse by bringing tins of sweets to the class. Sweets were rationed and in consequence he was regularly mobbed. It is important for the student teacher to come to a view about the use of Yorkie bars and 5p's as initial extrinsic motivators, not merely for their effect on the pupil but on the class as a whole. Many authorities would argue against the use of such incentives. The complete answers to the questions leave me with the clear impression that in the particular circumstances described they did work, and moreover, that the students enacted these situations with some caution.

These examples do illustrate the meanings of extrinsic and intrinsic motivation. Many other responses to the question cite the public examination as an important extrinsic motivator. As I have tried to show in both my books on examinations (*Examining in Second Level Education* and *Assessment in Higher Education*), examining and assessment systems can either impede (restrict) learning, or encourage learning to develop in specific and valued directions. I have been particularly concerned to develop procedures (see Chapter 7) which will achieve the latter end. There is no doubt that the teacher's aim should be to develop that curiosity in the subject which leads to learning for its own end, ie complete intrinsic motivation. However, the average pupil is unlikely to be equally interested in every subject. This is an important point, because many teachers would like to draw up profiles of student performances which would incorporate items in the affective domain. A good profile might be seen to be one in which a student is interested in every subject. This would be a very unfair judgement on the average student, however, for there are many factors which would militate against his or her being interested in every subject, not least for example his or her ability in subjects such as mathematics and languages. Students of low social class may be at a particular disadvantage, since their apparent lack of interest and ability may be a function of social class, as the first illustration below suggests. Nevertheless, this should not stop teachers from trying to stimulate curiosity in their subjects. There is some evidence, as the other answers below show, that some techniques of teaching encourage motivation more than others, although the use of such techniques may not mean that learning is as efficient as with other strategies. The project method is one such technique. The students wrote:

> In my own experience in a brand new Community School with just first-year students I had a marvellous opportunity to observe the different characteristics of the different classes. I taught four different classes — two 'bright', one remedial and one just above remedial.
> I observed that about half the school were motivated towards learning and the other half were not. This division almost perfectly correlated with their social class. I found this difficult to understand since I understood from my reading that motivation is intrinsic — sensory deprivation studies, and experiments with complex and simple stimuli plus the observations of people like Montessori all show this, and yet it was conspicuous by its absence in at least half the children — where had it all gone — this natural curiosity?
> Further reading told me that the children who gain most from the present system come from homes where education is valued for its own sake — where there are plenty of books and study is encouraged — ie closely tied up with parental approval. Another name would be 'conditioned'.

> Kersh also showed that the discovery method was not superior in retention or application but was significantly higher in motivation. And so, at present, guided discovery would have a relevant application in motivating a class. I have found this especially in the context of science. Instead of teaching a class how to test that chlorophyll is necessary for photosynthesis, I got the class to design an experiment themselves. Obviously, it is not practical, especially in one's HDip year, to allow the class to indulge in pure discovery, but it is important at least to allow them to discuss various possibilities. It gives them a greater appreciation of scientific method and of what scientific research is all about.

3.8 Tests, motivation and feedback

> In my dealings with children I try to arrange tests and questions in the classroom so that even the slow learners succeed at times. This has involved a task analysis and a breaking up of questions and tasks so that all can achieve success. Stars are an incentive to children. Receiving

a good grade is a rewarding experience for them.

Page has done research on the effects of writing comments on children's papers when handing back work. He maintains that spontaneous comments written by the teacher on the child's paper are an incentive to greater motivation. I have tried this out and found that the pupils seem to enjoy getting a good comment and respond better to this than merely writing a per cent mark or an 'A' or 'B', etc, on their papers.

When teachers set questions either by the spoken word in the class, or in written form in homework or examinations, they are setting goals which have to be achieved. The questions are a source of motivation. If a child is persistently asked questions which are too difficult, he or she is likely to become depressed. Most of us do not, by and large, perform very well when we are depressed. Many children arriving for a particular class may dread being asked a question by that teacher for fear not only that they will not be able to answer the question but of the retribution which will follow. That particular teacher has not created a classroom climate conducive to learning.

The same applies, as the second quotation above shows, to the return of homework and the use of grades. Many pupils find essay-writing difficult. One reason for this is that they may never have been shown how to write an essay. Of course the organization, structure and approach will vary from subject to subject but in the later years of secondary education there is a greater need for deliberate training in the construction of essays within the particular subject taught. This would comprise instruction with the aid of examples on the logical structure of the essays together with feedback on essays produced by the pupils. (I have discussed the potential for this kind of training in *Assessment in Higher Education*, pp 30-43.) The essay marking scheme (Exhibit 3.2) illustrates the general idea. The point to emerge is that if the student does not understand the meaning of logical structure, specific training is required. Too often, as when using mediating responses, the teacher assumes that the student has unconsciously grasped the meaning of logical structure. Students will become depressed if they cannot see what they can do to improve their performance.

3.9 Personality, achievement and motivation

The postulates on extrinsic and intrinsic motivation have to be modified by the fact that personality intervenes to influence motivation. In this section we look at three aspects — anxiety, introversion and extroversion, and achievement motivation.

(a) Anxiety and intelligence

A number of experiments have been carried out which relate anxiety to intelligence. They do not show that anxiety is necessarily harmful to learning, although there are certainly individuals who when faced with

---

Iliffe's suggested guide for the marking of essays

% *Reason for mark*

80 Outstanding answer: shows independent reading and thinking

70 Best possible organization of all expected material

60 Well organized use of most major points

50 Sensible use of some major points

45 Clear signs of understanding, but material thin

(pass)

40 Some relevant material but incomplete grasp

30 Not an answer to the question set, but shows some understanding
    of the general field

20 Very muddled, but shows some understanding of the general field

10 Poorly organized and almost completely lacking in relevance

---

Exhibit 3.2 *Essay marking scheme.* (In Iliffe and Heywood, 1966)

tests become so anxious about failing and the consequences of failure that they give poor responses to questions. But anxiety and arousal are also related, and known to improve the test performance of some individuals. Research into this aspect of test performance treats anxiety as a personality trait. But anxiety may be a state of mind as well as a personality trait, and may set up defence mechanisms to avoid itself. The state and the trait are of course related. Anxiety treated as arousal is a state: one investigation has shown that when students are aroused, high anxiety students do well when relatively few recall errors are possible. In contrast, when a larger number of recall errors are allowed, low anxiety students obtain better results (Spielberger, 1966). In the middle range of intelligence, low anxiety students performed better than high anxiety students, but high anxiety did not affect the performance of low ability students. Low anxiety students are better at rote learning than high anxiety students, and high anxiety, high intelligence students are better at learning concepts than low anxiety, high intelligence students. The more anxious the low intelligence student the less likely he is to do well when learning concepts. In so far as the highly able students are concerned, the long term effects of anxiety are such that the least anxious do better.

(b) Temperament and examination performance

Some light is thrown on these studies by an investigation of engineering students at a college in England by Furneaux (1962). He used a personality test which assessed introversion and extroversion along one dimension, and neuroticism (or stability) along the other.

The results showed that after the first year in college neurotic-introverts did better than stable-introverts, neurotic-extroverts and stable-extroverts in that order. Sixty per cent of the stable-extroverts failed. There are several more recent studies of this kind. Furneaux's study is of interest because of the explanation which he offers.

When a person is in a state of arousal he is said to be in a condition of high drive. It has been shown by Yerkes and Dodson (using animals) that the more hungry a rat the more quickly it will learn to traverse a maze to obtain food (see Broadhurst, 1959). Increasing the hunger has the effect of increasing the drive. But in their experiments Yerkes and Dodson found there is an optimum level of drive beyond which performance falls. This level is high for simple tasks and low for complex tasks. Furneaux explained his results in terms of this theory.

First, it is postulated that persons who enter easily into high drive states are more likely to obtain high neuroticism scores than those whose drive levels are generally low. A test of neuroticism is therefore a test of habitual drive level. The argument which follows is that a person who has a low drive level and who is also extroverted will only do well if he has above average intelligence.

Second, Furneaux found that there was one examination in which the high drive neurotic-introverts did not do as well as those with a habitual low level of drive. This was in the engineering drawing examination. Furneaux postulates that this is an examination where the Yerkes-Dodson optimum occurs at a relatively low level of drive. Since the high drive students exceed this level they do badly. During the examination they may sweat, tremble and make poor judgements. In this case they presented poor drawings which showed 'all the signs of disturbing influences'. Changes in the drawing examination led to positive changes in performance among the less stable groups, a result which seems to confirm the theory.

The situation is further complicated by the fact that the situations which put a person into a high drive differ between the groups. Inter-personal relationships may not send a neurotic-introvert into a state of high drive whereas they will have that effect on a neurotic-extrovert. Thus a neurotic-extrovert, because of supra-optimal drive, may well fail a selection interview. Furneaux found that neurotic-extroverts were selected by the college in 'proportionately, rather small numbers, although the effect was not very large'.

All these results suggest that groups of university students or pupils in a class should not be treated homogeneously. Combinations of coursework assessment and examinations are to be preferred to examinations if this is the general case, and the need for counselling among university students would seem to be self-evident. In schools, as the response on p 52 shows, some children are taken aside: but it is possible that many children who have learning difficulties arising from temperament go through school and college without an awareness that they have such difficulties. The case for instruction on 'learning how to learn' among older pupils is strong.

(c) Achievement motivation

McClelland (1953) and co-workers developed a substantial research programme around the concept of *achievement motivation* (expectancy of
finding satisfaction in mastering challenging and difficult tasks which are
realistic to the person involved). They believe that there is a need for
achievement in each individual which, although internal to the individual,
is affected by the culture in which a person lives. For some years they have
been implementing programmes for the development of the achievement
motive in businessmen. They believe that many pupils in schools can be
oriented towards achievement by their teachers. The problem is to develop
the existing entering characteristics so that the students will undertake
more challenging problems.

De Cecco and Crawford (1974) conclude their discussion of achievement motivation with this quotation from the philosopher William James
(1892):

> Pugnacity need not be thought of merely in the form of physical
> combativeness. It can be taken in the sense of general unwillingness to
> be beaten by any kind of difficulty. It is what makes us feel 'stumped'
> and challenged by arduous achievements, and is essential to a spirited
> and enterprising character. We have of late been hearing much of the
> philosophy of tenderness in education; 'interest' must be assiduously
> awakened in everything, and difficulties must be smoothed away.
> *Soft* pedagogics have taken the place of the old steep and rocky path
> to learning. But from this lukewarm air the bracing oxygen of effort is
> left out. It is nonsense to suppose that every step in education *can* be
> interesting. The fighting impulse must often be appealed to. Make the
> pupil feel ashamed of being scared of fractions, of being 'downed' by
> the law of falling bodies; arouse his pugnacity and pride, and he will
> rush at the difficult places with an inner wrath at himself that is one of
> his best faculties . . . . The teacher who never rouses this sort of
> pugnacious excitement in his pupils falls short of one of his best forms
> of usefulness.

3.10 Concluding remarks

It is appropriate to conclude this chapter with an extensive quotation from
one of the answers to the questions set. It is given not least for the limited
feedback which it offers but as much for the examples it gives, which
show clearly the need for teachers to come to grips with the problem of
motivation.

> Educational research on motivation can help the teacher not only
> realize its importance but give him/her clues as to what techniques
> to use in teaching. Firstly it shows the importance of seeing each
> child as an individual and assessing the entering behaviour of each:
> influences on motivation come from many sources — the society, home

background, school, class group, past success and failure, personality relationship with the teacher. A knowledge of the influence of all these factors on the child's attitude to learning can give the teacher insight into why he is/isn't motivated to learn and what to do about it: eg a child may see no value in academic achievement yet have the intellectual ability to learn well ('under-achievers'); another may have a high valence but not expect to learn anything due to past failure, low IQ, etc.

There are two particular cases in my former class which fit these in part. Both Lisa-Anne and Cathy have caused a lot of problems, disrupting the class with arguments and smart comments. Cathy, I was told by many teachers in the school is just 'stupid', she hasn't the ability to learn much. I presume the fact that Cathy has developed a self-image of being stupid but amusing makes her seek her attention/popularity through being comical and even accentuating her stupid remarks in class. I had the chance of giving her some extra private lessons (since she had missed a few classes due to illness before Christmas) and found that when I had taken her slowly through the steps she was able to learn quite well how to tell the time in German. Giving easy problems first and then difficult ones led her from success to success and developed her confidence that she *could* do the work. The research on the influence of success and failure on pupils' achievement is extremely useful — it points out that constant failure will result in either the pupil lowering or giving up his expectations of success, or raising them to an unrealistically high level as if the hope of success alone might bring it. This latter is exactly what Cathy tended to do — putting up her hand to answer questions that she couldn't answer correctly, and then often arguing with me that she was right (substituting the goal of getting attention and a laugh from the others in the class for the goal of the correct answer). After the private classes her performance in class improved markedly and it is a pity I haven't had the chance to devote more time to her individual case to keep up this development.

Lisa-Anne on the other hand is what is called an 'under-achiever' — I tried for a long time encouraging her, then giving out to her, moving her to the front row, but nothing worked. It was only when we started doing role-playing and drama that she became interested. I also found out that she was extremely interested in baking and at Christmas asked her to bake some German recipes for the class which proved a huge success. I was acting here on intuition and on having read Erich Berne's work on Transactional Analysis which was extremely useful in getting through the psychological games that were going on, preventing learning.

Although educational research holds many clues to help the teacher it does not have any definite answers, and it may be necessary to combine a few theories of behaviour to find out why a child is being disruptive, etc. If he is looking for attention it may be possible to give this in other ways than by giving out to him, etc. In any case the research gives the teacher many different viewpoints from which to look at the situation and helps him in reaching the right conclusion or at least involves him in the complexity of causes behind seemingly simple acts.

Notes and references

E Berne (1970) *The Psychology of Human Relationships*. Harmondsworth: Penguin.
P L Broadhurst (1959) The interaction of task difficulty and motivation: the Yerkes-Dodson law revived, *Acta Psychol.*, 16, 321-38.
H F Clarizio (1971) *Toward Positive Classroom Discipline*. New York: Wiley.
J C Coleman (1950) *Abnormal Psychology and Modern Life*. New York: Scott Foresman.
J P de Cecco and W R Crawford (1974) *The Psychology of Learning and Instruction*. Englewood Cliffs, NJ: Prentice-Hall.
W W Daniel and N McIntosh (1972) *The Right to Manage*. London: Macdonald and Janes.
B Engler (1979) *Personality Theories. An Introduction*. Boston, Mass: Houghton Mifflin.
E Frenkel-Brunswick (1942) Motivation and behaviour, *Genetic Psychology Monographs*, 26, 121-265.
W D Furneaux (1962) The psychologist and the university, *Universities Quarterly*, 17, 33-47.
D O Hebb (1955) Drives and the conceptual nervous system. *Psychological Review*, 62, 243.
J Heywood (1978) *Examining in Second Level Education*. Dublin: ASTI.
A H Iliffe and J Heywood (eds) (1966) *Some Aspects of Testing for Academic Performance*. Bulletin No 2, Department of Higher Education, University of Lancaster.
W James (1892) *Talks to Teachers on Psychology and to Students on Some of Life's Ideals*. New York: Norton.
R S Lazarus (1965) *Personality and Adjustment*. Englewood Cliffs, NJ: Prentice-Hall.
A H Maslow (1943) A theory of human motivation, *Psychological Review*, 50, 370-96.
D C McClelland, J W Atkinson, R A Clark and E L Lowell (1953) *The Achievement Motive*. New York: Appleton-Century-Crofts.
F J McDonald (1965) *Educational Psychology*. Belmont, Cal: Wadsworth.
E J Murray (1965) *Motivation and Emotion*. Englewood Cliffs, NJ: Prentice-Hall.
H A Murray (1938) *Explorations in Personality*. New York: Oxford University Press.
C B Patterson (1977) *Foundations for a Theory of Instruction and Educational Psychology*. New York: Harper & Row. (See especially Chapter 5: Skinner and the technology of teaching.)
J Powell (1978) *Unconditional Love*. Illinois: Argus.
E H Schein (1966) *Organizational Psychology*. Englewood Cliffs, NJ: Prentice-Hall.
L S Shulman (1970) Psychology and mathematics education, in E G Begle (ed) *Mathematics Education*. Chicago, Ill: National Society for the Study of Education/University of Chicago Press.
C D Spielberger (1966) in C D Spielberger (ed) *Anxiety and Behaviour*. New York: Academic Press.

Terminology

Engler's book contains a useful glossary of terms as do McDonald, Cohen and Mannion (see references to Chapter 1), Lazarus, and E J Murray.

4 Perception

4.1 Organizing questions

1. In what ways should teachers be influenced by perceptual learning theory? Indicate with examples its possible implications for the subject you teach.

2. In what way should the perceptual learning theories of such writers as Abercrombie, Hesseling and Solly influence the way you think about your pupils (or) make you hesitate before you make the statement, 'I "know" all about that pupil.' Illustrate your answer by references to your own inter-actions with pupils in the classroom.

3. How would you advise a student teacher to make the best of his/her observations of other teachers at work?

4. 'Liberal education might be described as the provision of the widest range of schemata (frames of reference).' How does perceptual learning theory support this view? In what ways do you seek to overcome 'bias' in the subject you teach?

5. 'Our basic postulate is that human behaviour can be explained by this underlying perceptual process. Changing a person's behaviour is changing his perceptual strategies. Strategies alter with the nature of the task, the definition of the situation and expected consequences of behaviour' (Hesseling, 1966).

   Having defined strategies, situation and consequences of behaviour in relation to pupil learning, illustrate from your teaching experience the significance or otherwise of this hypothesis for pupil learning.

6. Discuss the relevance of perceptual learning theory in the education and training of the slow learner.

4.2 Organizing answers

1. There are four major factors that influence our perceptual learning: our limited capacity or experience of the world; categories or concepts we have already formed by which we classify our experience; bias or prejudice towards particular situations, things or people; meaning that we attach to our experience which is totally personal and subjective . . .

Firstly their experience of the world is limited. Many slow learners come from deprived social backgrounds. Teachers should attempt to widen the span of their experience by organizing trips and camping out project work designed to do this. This must be done, however, without inciting their bias by making them feel inferior or ashamed of their limitations.

Secondly, a major problem with slow learners, may be the result of the difference between their categorization and the teacher's. We must beware of over-categorizing to produce stereotypes. Deprived children may place school and prison in the same category and teachers have to try to break down categories to help the pupils form new ones, to advance and progress towards new fields of knowledge.

2. I shall now detail two difficulties in perception which it has been noticed are common among slow learners in mathematics.

With regard to right-angled triangles — such pupils always expect the orientation (a) but if presented as in (b) they do not recognize it as such.

(a)   (b)

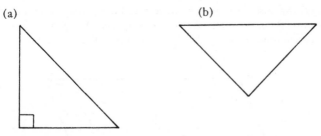

Another example would be to present a rectangle and a parallelogram thus:

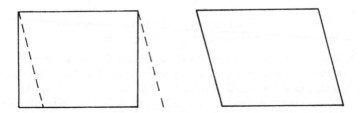

and suggest that the areas might be the same. The slow learner will invariably dispute this.

This shows an inadequate entering behaviour, which shows that previously 'learned' concepts have been incorrectly formed, and learned.

3. Mathematics involves a tremendous amount of visual ability and the children should be given a good training in this area. Perception theory helps us to communicate the mathematical work in a manner which not only examines the maths but which also helps to develop the child's perception of the world and of this experience. In the previous case of parallel projection I can relate a number of incidences which caused me to take perception more seriously into focus. I usually presented parallel projection in the manner represented in the diagram. The parallel projection was always

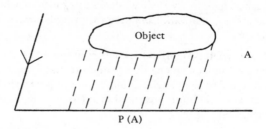

P (A)

subconsciously in the same position and it was only when I came to proving theorems later on that they emerged. The proof of the theorem required the parallel direction as in the diagram on

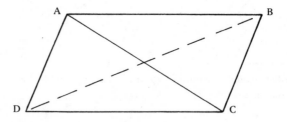

(AC) // (BD). This was a new problem in perception for the children and a new interest in perceptual training for me.

4. The reason I talk to them in parables is that they look without seeing and listen without hearing or understanding. So in their case this prophecy of Isaiah is being fulfilled: You will listen and listen again, but not understand, see and see again, but not perceive. For the heart of this nation has grown coarse, their ears are dull of hearing, and they have shut their eyes for fear they should see with their eyes, hear with their ears, understand with their hearts, and be converted and be healed by me. 'But happy are your eyes because they see, your ears because they hear.' I tell you solemnly, many prophets and holy men longed to see what you see, and never saw it; to hear what you hear, and never heard it. (St Matthew 13: 13-17)

4.3 Seeing is believing

For a number of years I gave student engineers and teachers, to whom I was to give a programme in behavioural science, a so-called psychological test. They were told that the purpose of the exercise was (1) to show them the importance of standardization when setting tests (ie standardization of procedures so that a test is always set in the same way), (2) to illustrate objective items, and (3) to illustrate a test which was culture-free. They were also told that I would not look at individual scores.

They were required to give one answer only to questions about a number of pictures presented on the screen in the lecture theatre. Another important instruction was to the effect that the test would be done at speed since speed of performance is related to intelligence. Several repetitions were made of the point that there was only one right answer to the question.

A typical question is shown in Exhibit 4.1. If you look at it quickly you will probably think that line 'b' is longer than line 'a'. However, both

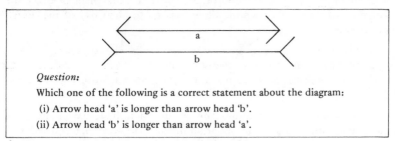

Question:

Which one of the following is a correct statement about the diagram:

(i) Arrow head 'a' is longer than arrow head 'b'.

(ii) Arrow head 'b' is longer than arrow head 'a'.

Exhibit 4.1

lines are, in fact, the same length. This is an optical illusion known as the Müller-Lyer illusion. To their annoyance, most of the class answered either (i) or (ii) depending on where they were sitting in the lecture theatre.

I do the same thing with several other pictures, which come from a book by Jane Abercrombie (1960) called *The Anatomy of Judgement*. One shows three men in a tube; to most people all the men seem to be of different sizes. In fact, they are all the same size. There is also a black-and-white diagram, which the test question suggests could represent snow on a mountain, an inkblot test sheet, or a young child's drawing. When we turn over the page in Jane Abercrombie's book we find that it was a picture of a prophet or Christ. Jane Abercrombie writes about the first picture thus:

> The face may appear as suddenly as when a light has been switched on. Some people cannot see it with the help of words only, but need someone to trace the outline features over the patchwork. The object has not changed, nor has its image on the retina, yet the information received from the object is different — no longer is it seen as a chaotic patchwork, but as the picture of a man, sharp and clear and characteristic.

My first aim in setting these tests was to remove the prejudice which students so often bring to the study of the social and behavioural sciences, ie that they know how people behave. The test experience is intended to reinforce the open-mindedness with which they should approach any study. Second, and much more important, is the generalization of that principle that beauty is in the eye of the beholder. The hidden man pictures demonstrate that what is perceived depends not only on what is being looked at but on the state of the perceiver. The perceiver brings something to the act of knowledge as well as the object of knowledge itself. What the perceiver brings may 'colour' considerably what is seen. Third, I aimed to show that without some prior frame of reference related to the subject under consideration it is very difficult to understand new material; fourth, and most important, that it is very easy to be deceived; and fifth, I aimed to introduce perceptual learning theory.

My impression from discussion with students after the lectures was that other aims are achieved. I would say that the second aim above is probably next in importance to the fourth, if I had to rank them in order. In summary, the aim of presenting these tests on the first day of the course was to show:

1. that things in a classroom may not always be what they seem;
2. that communication is a two-way affair;
3. that communicators do not always perceive each other in the same way.

Translated into teaching terms, this means that, first, the pupils (or a pupil) may not 'see' your information in the same way that you yourself see it. If this is the case there will be a communication gap. Lack of understanding by pupils may well be caused by your conduct, eg presentation, time allowed for cogitation, etc (see section 4.7).

Second, first impressions of a pupil may not be the correct impressions of that child. It is, for example, particularly difficult not to be influenced by teachers' remarks in the staffroom about a pupil you have seen. Take time to get to know your pupils, and take time and care with your presentations. Two-way communication is not a simple affair.

Third, since the way in which we perceive is at the basis of all communications it is fundamental to life. It is arguable that problems in trade union negotiations (see Chapter 2, p 33) arise from the different perceptions that the negotiators have of one another's stance. Riots like those in Toxteth, Liverpool and Brixton were due in no small measure to the differing perceptions of individuals and individual rights held by the police on the one hand, and the members of the community on the other. Perhaps the best example of differing perceptions and their likely effects is to be found in the parable of the sower in St Matthew — the fourth of the organizing answers given above. In the sections which follow, we look first at some of the factors which influence perception, and second, at the development of perceptual motor learning and its influence on ability. There is a tendency among student teachers to be excited by the latter and to ignore the former. This means they overlook the hypotheses stated above, which probably means that they overlook them in their everyday affairs often to the cost of interpersonal relations (see also p 95).

4.4 Factors influencing perception

What we perceive depends not only on what is to be perceived but on the state of the perceiver and whether the perceiver is internally organized to perceive. The theory of perceptual motor development, which is dealt with in the last section of this chapter, argues that the sequence of perceptual development is important: if it gets out of order learning disabilities may arise. We cannot say for certain how perceptual development generally takes place, but we can make some reasonable hypotheses.

In order to interpret the outer world we must have some internal 'frames of reference' (variously called schemata, schema, and categories), against which to make an association. These help us to relate old information with new information. Abercrombie (1960) says that they may 'be regarded as tools which help us to see, evaluate and respond'. Another famous psychologist, G Allport (1961), writes of categories which are accessible clusters of associated ideas in our mind; these serve as a frame of reference for fresh perceptual samples of immediate modes of behaviour. Hesseling (1966) wrote:

> The working of these schemata can be indirectly observed in everyday experience. For example when we instructed a group of chargehands during a residential course to observe accurately and in detail some charwoman cleaning up the house, they reported individually the observed behaviour in terms of work methods, tools, performance and similar categories. They used these categories in their daily work and they expected to be asked for such observations in this training situation. They did not observe this behaviour. Much socio-psychological research demonstrates an inner consistency among an individual's perceptions and his needs, his values, his cognitive style and way of looking at life.

We can argue that one effect of the restricted code of speech (see notes to Chapter 2) is to limit the acquisition of categories. We can also argue that the life styles associated with the different economic groups provide different internal structures (frames of reference), and that these differences lead to differences in perception which create communication barriers between the groups.

Notice too how training can influence structure. Often highly specialized and highly qualified persons working in the same factory cannot understand each other because they do not comprehend the language of one another's specialization. The ways in which lawyers and engineers look at an aircraft which has crashed due to metal fatigue are totally different. They may well have difficulty in communicating with each other. I have argued in *Analysing Jobs* (Youngman *et al*, 1978) that too much experience can militate against innovation. We tend to rely on experience. We do not like going outside the realms of the familiar. I have also argued that the theory of perceptual learning leads to a view of liberal education as that process which provides a person with the widest possible range of frames of reference together with the learning skills necessary for problem solving at the highest levels of mental and moral development.

It should be evident that we cannot cope with all the information available to us: we have to select. This selection will be influenced by our internal structure, which includes our intelligence, aptitudes and interests. But because we collect information from our particular environment, it too influences our selection: some environments are very limiting. This is yet another way of accounting for the learning differences between the socioeconomic classes. Clearly the acquisition of such different perceptions has within it the seeds of conflict.

Also influencing the acquisition of information is bias (prejudice), ie the tendency to favour and support a point of view or conclusion despite the absence of adequate or even any evidence. We all have such dispositions, a major influence on which is our personality. An authoritarian personality is likely to be 'closed' to new experiences (Adorno, 1950). At the other end of the spectrum are those persons who often restructure their experience. The significance of such dispositions is illustrated in many spheres of life: the 1981 riots in England and the friction between the two communities in Northern Ireland provide good but sad examples.

One of our student respondents wrote:

> My own experience has shown me that (a) *convergent thinkers* when faced with a 'hard' question (in Irish) will refuse to write anything or attempt the question, if they are not confident that they have the right answer, while (b) *divergent thinkers* are inclined to have a 'bash' at the question. (Pugnacity?)

Hudson (1966) has so popularized the concept of convergent and divergent thinking that there should be little need to paraphrase that limited description.

We also impose *meaning* on the objects and events which surround us. To take another example from Hesseling:

> We can find in common experience many examples of the different meaning attached to specific behaviour. A student had to make a sampling study of chargehands in a fairly confined factory, without complete introduction. He started on a Monday morning. A new product was now assembled and production was under time stress. Because he often spoke to the chargehands and was continually making notes, he appeared to most of the young assembly workers as a controller of their bosses. His appearance near their assembly lines was welcomed with some satisfaction: they became bolder towards the chargehands, made jokes and nudged each other when he was

approaching. To the chargehands he seemed a menace: they became uncertain and nervous and they concerned themselves more with the production process itself than with their group of workers. To the departmental manager he became a scapegoat: he blamed several production faults on this work sampling study and he walked about in the factory more than usual.

This example also serves to illustrate the role of aims and objectives in removing ambiguity from teaching. Much misunderstanding in life and learning, as Woodhouse (1979) has pointed out, arises from the fact that the learner (worker, individual) perceives the situation to be ambiguous. For example, it was very clear in June 1981 when the railway unions and the Railway Board in Britain sought the help of the Advisory, Conciliation, and Arbitration Service that their agreement was ambiguous. One union said that it had not related the award to productivity. The Board said it had. They both maintained these positions, and the result was a strike in 1982.

Aims and objectives provide a focus for the drive which leads to further insight and understanding. The example in Exhibit 4.2 should suffice to illustrate this point.

The obligations that perceptual learning places on a teacher are considerable. First, he must ensure that his sampling of events, particularly of pupil behaviour in the classroom, is a broad as possible, before he arrives at a percept. Second, he must try to minimize the number of wrong schemata before the percept is formed and accepted. Third, he must be open to and test different possibilities in order to prevent bias. Fourth, he must ensure that he reaches a percept which could be expected by others in a given situation.

In planning a lesson he will be greatly helped by the aims and objectives approach which is set out in detail in Chapter 8. In so doing he should take into account that the pupils have a perception of him, and that this is of importance to their performance. This aspect of classroom behaviour is considered in the next section.

4.5 Objectivity

Despite the fact that I spend a lot of time on the problems of perception, students find it a hard lesson to learn if they learn it at all. When they come on their initial training course, for example, many of them believe that it is not possible to use any of the methods of teaching suggested in this book because coverage of the examination syllabus will not allow them the time required for such refinements. Syndicate methods within large lectures followed by discussion and illustration do not seem to make them any less closed-minded. (Closed and open-mindedness are personality dimensions similar to the authoritarian-democratic dimensions — see Rokeach, 1960.)

I am sure that most teachers would argue that they do not have likes and dislikes. Yet the evidence is that they do. In *Classrooms Observed,*

**AIMS AND OBJECTIVES OF INTERMEDIATE CERTIFICATE
FOR THE 1976 EXAMINATION**

Knowledge and comprehension

Pupils should be able to recall, recognize and understand the principal events, trends and issues of the periods of history set out in the syllabus. They should have some understanding of the recent evolution of the world in which they live.

Skills

Pupils should be able to practise, at a level suitable to their stage of development, the skills used in history, more particularly:

  (i) the ability to locate, understand and record simple historical information; and

  (ii) the ability to examine critically and discuss statements on historical matters encountered in their textbooks and in everyday life.

Pupils should feel a responsibility:

  (i) to be objective in interpreting historical material;

  (ii) to find rational explanations for historical events and developments;

  (iii) to understand what it is like to be in someone else's position;

  (iv) to respect the right of others to be different and to hold different points of view.

Pupils should be encouraged to value their heritage from the past.

Exhibit 4.2

a book which ought to be read by all student teachers, Roy Nash (1973) gives two examples which demonstrate this point. First, he found that pupils who were assigned to a remedial class after their first term in a second level school were perceived less favourably by teachers than many others in the same group of pupils, even though the others had comparable IQs and positions in their primary school classes. Nash argues that despite the fact that teachers say they do not have likes and dislikes, they behave as if they do. There is a refusal to recognize that just as in their everyday relationships with adults they can behave in ways for which they cannot account, so they can have irrational reactions to their pupils. The solution might be to transfer such pupils to another teacher if possible, rather than to a remedial class.

It does not take long to find out from a group of children that some of them get on with Teacher X while others do not. More important is the fact that some will in all probability believe that their learning difficulties arise because of their relationship with Teacher X. However, the fact that teachers in Nash's study saw pupils as much in terms of their personality as their academic ability has its positive side as well as its negative.

Nash's second example of faulty judgement relates to beliefs about social class and performance. He found that teachers who thought social class a determinant of ability often made wrong judgements about children. Pupils who were slower and less likeable than others were thought to come from the lower social classes. In reality this was not true: these pupils had similar backgrounds to the others. The teachers' assumptions may have arisen from an over-emphasis of the findings of sociology that low ability and low social class correlate. Teachers should not assume, however, that this will always be the case.

How, then, can objectivity be acquired? There is no simple answer to this question. One might begin with the salutary reminder, to be found in other reports as well as Nash's, *that your pupils are not only making judgements about you, but they are also working out what you think of them, and that this judgement will be an important determinant of the achievement of many of them.* Children in unstreamed primary classes may know their position in the class; their perceptions of you may also be right. Knowledge of our own personality disposition is therefore of considerable value.

Microteaching should help with the development of the skill of 'personal objectivity', but it cannot assess performance in the classroom. A better method is to be regularly assessed in the classroom by another teacher who has been trained in the observation of classroom behaviour. A promising approach suggested by Flanders, one of the pioneers of inter-action analysis (see notes at the end of this chapter), is for student teachers to work in pairs: one would observe while the other teaches and vice-versa, and prior training would be given in the techniques of observation. This approach is being developed in the School of Education at the University of Nottingham. Finally, a knowledge of the techniques used by research workers to observe classrooms should help teachers to understand better the needs of the classroom and sensitize them to the organization in which they work.

This is by no means all there is to perception for it is the way in which we, when infants, perceive our bodies that is the beginning of learning. We will now consider perceptual motor development and its implications for learning among the less able.

4.6 Perceptual training in the curriculum: an insight

Many dyslexic children, eg perceive letters and sentences in quite a different frame of references from the normal child. Therefore much work on visual perception must be completed before reading of any kind can begin. Likewise with writing many children who have difficulties with spatial perception cannot write until a good deal of work has been completed in spatial relations, eg drawing figures, eg square. However, perceptual training exercises such as plotting the route from school to home, home to school can be useful.

Few of our student teachers give examples of perceptual learning theory applied to the solution of learning disorders in the classroom. It is an area which is introduced in our course but not developed. Most students find it fascinating.

G H Early (1969) argues that many learning disorders occur because of perceptual problems. More often than not these occur because the pupil has not progressed through the stages of perceptual development satisfactorily. Early tries to show how the curriculum can be used to remedy these defects.

In order to receive and organize information from the outside world, human beings have to be organized and structured internally. They need, for example, an inner awareness of 'left' and 'right'. Without this, they may confuse the letters 'b' and 'd'. Similarly, if they are not aware of 'up' and 'down' they may not be able to distinguish 'p' from 'd'. These examples are commonplace. Something, argues Early, is wrong with their internal structure because they do not see what we see. When we come across a child with acute reading difficulties, therefore, it might be sensible to see if they can make these distinctions. What does the child see when he reads? is a useful organizing question since it places our thoughts within the perspective of the child.

How then does a child develop its internal structure? Clearly, it arises from an inter-action with the world in which he lives. And these inter-actions begin from 0 + 1.

> As a simple example of how internal organization is used to organize incoming information, consider a child as he looks at a tree some 50 or so feet from himself. He knows the direction to the tree only because he knows the direction in which his head and eyes are pointing. He knows the direction of his head and eyes only from his internal structure. His neck muscles produce information about the location of his eyes with respect to his head. Since he is organized internally, this information from these particular muscles tells him the direction of his gaze. Without this internal organization he will not know with accuracy where his eyes are pointing, and so will lack essential information for learning relationships among objects in space. (Early, 1969)

The process by which this internal structure is developed may be called perceptual motor development. The stages are as follows:

1. Motor level
2. Motor perceptual level
3. Perceptual motor level
4. Perceptual level
5. Perceptual conceptual level
6. Conceptual level
7. Conceptual perceptual level.

An infant functions at the motor level. His own movements produce internal information. The central nervous system receives continuous information about the position of the body parts. This information becomes structured and provides frames of reference against which further action can be checked. It is this internal reference system which is called the motor base. It only becomes fully organized when it uses visual and aural information. It begins by separating out the body parts in two directions: first, from the centre of the body outwards, and second, from head to toe. There is a sequential development, and if the sequence is not followed learning disorders may arise. Kephart (1960) and Early have given examples of how teachers can impede this development. For example, if an infant teacher tries to make a child draw with a crayon before it can differentiate its hand, wrist, elbow and arm it will force its fingers to draw but the drawing will be characterized by rigidity. The child learns an isolated (or splinter as they are termed) skill. Such skills are not related to the motor base. Early describes a nine-year-old who when writing at a chalk board kept his whole arm rigid: the writing movements were made from the shoulder, because he was not able to differentiate the parts of his arm. Children need to (and normal children do) develop generalized movement patterns. This provides them with an awareness of their potential for movement at any given time.

All positions in the universe are relative. There is no absolute right or left, top or bottom: these are relative to the person who is making the measurement. We arrive at our definition of left and right by using our body as the reference point: left and right derive from *laterality* in the motor base. This is developed as we solve problems. As in so many activities, the child can often name left and right without understanding them. Experience is required for much understanding.

Up and down are defined from *verticality* in the motor base. From the need to describe our body we arrive at left and right by dividing it into two lateral halves, up and down, by dividing the body into upper and lower halves and front and rear (behind), ie mentally allowing the body to be divided by a vertical plane.

Information is also received from the eyes. Hand-eye co-ordination is of considerable importance. One often sees highly intelligent people whose hand-eye co-ordination appears to be lacking when they use psychomotor skills: the sequence is hand-eye, eye-hand (stages 2 and 3). Observe how the infant's eye is attracted to the hand: it is only later that the child realizes that there are two sources of information about the same event. Sound also comes to be recognized as a source of information.

Geography is an invaluable subject for the development of both visual observation and hand-eye co-ordination skills. Some idea of its potential is given below. Moreover, at higher levels it requires the development of very complex skills in such things as the analysis of aerial photographs. At the elementary level pupils have to learn to use simple measuring devices.

When perception (stage 4) has developed the motor aspect drops out, and the information is organized directly. Early quotes the example of reading the lines of a book. To illustrate the role of perception, close your eyes and see if you can locate in your mind all the objects in the room you are in. The final stage of development is when previously learned concepts condition perception.

Time also has to be structured. Children whose time world is not structured will try to do everything immediately. In order to be able to draw a square they have to have a time structure. If they do not they try to solve everything by very rapid movements, and in so doing lose the whole. Children therefore need a time structure if they are to sequence activities. The components of time structure are synchrony (purposeful simultaneity of movement), rhythm, and sequence.

Early argues that failure to develop a solid internal structure will lead to learning difficulties. Several tests have been developed which may help teachers overcome this kind of impediment (Roach and Kephart, 1966). Most of Early's book is devoted to examples (in science, languages and social studies) of how the curriculum can help such training. One of these is a social studies project for low ability (under-achieving, slow learning) American fifth-graders. The project included the construction of a geographical globe, floor map and time line on a very big scale. The globe, for example, was nearly as big as the children. When it was in use, the children could learn about the relations among objects in space as well as spatial and temporal operations.

Early claims that the construction of the globe will cater for the following perceptual developments:

Construction Phase — Constructing the Globe Map.
1. Making styrofoam rings (which will be formed into the sphere).
   (a) *Perceptual-motor Matching:* Sawing concentric rings from styrofoam gives simultaneous visual, auditory, and tactual-kinesthetic feedback.
   (b) *Differentiation:* Feedback promotes awareness of parts used in the task.
   (c) *Integration:* Co-ordinated movements are developed. Control of movement is developed.
   (d) *Generalization:* Different sizes of rings are made, thus varying the movements involved.
2. Assembling styrofoam rings into outline of sphere.
   Form Perception: Parts are assembled into a whole. Motor and visual activity are both involved; the child *experiences* the whole coming together from the parts.
3. Making the globe surface with papier-maché clay.
   (a) *Perceptual-motor Matching:* Visual and tactual-kinesthetic feedback comes from hands spreading clay.
   (b) *Differentiation:* Clay gives unique tactual-kinesthetic feedback which promotes awareness of those parts involved in the task.
   (c) *Integration:* Two hands and arms work together in spreading clay; co-ordination and control are developed.
   (d) *Generalization:* Working on top, bottom, and sides requires different body positions and much variety of muscle combinations to do the same task.

4. Locating North and South Poles.
   (a) *Directionality, Spatial Relations:* North Pole is located by children observing (from a distance) and pointing to high point on globe; motor is involved with visual in indicating relations.
   (b) *Generalization:* South Pole location involves same task, but radically different body positions and movements.
5. Locating and drawing equator, lines of longitude and latitude, and outlines of land masses.
   (a) *Perceptual-motor Matching:* Globe surface is rough sand finish; drawing is done with charcoal pencil. Drawing thus provides visual, auditory, and tactual-kinesthetic feedback.
   (b) *Differentiation:* See preceding sections on differentiation.
   (c) *Integration:* See preceding sections on integration.
   (d) *Generalization:* Task requires variety of body movements and muscle combinations.
   (e) *Form Perception:* Whole is *experienced* from visual, auditory, and tactual-kinesthetic involvement of child with parts.
   (Early, 1969: pp 36-7)

The reader is referred to a more recent work by Ainscow and Tweddle (1979) for a brief introduction to the design of lesson programmes for perceptual motor development using the objectives approach.

4.7 Teaching and perceptual learning

The perceptual process is closely related to motivation, for our desires, experience and knowledge combine to evaluate events and create expectancies. The act of forming a percept can be conceived as a progressive activity involving expectation, attention, reception, trial and error checking, leading to the formation of a perception, and subsequently to behavioural and cognitive activity in which experience develops new and reorganizes old responses. The perceptual act restructures our world.

The stage of expectancy was discussed in the last chapter. Our expectancies are, of course, influenced by numerous factors; but we need them in order to organize incoming information. In doing this, it seems that we remember past successes and ignore past failures. Once again the importance of success (success breeding success) is emphasized. Expectancy is also influenced by persistent modes of problem solving which we learn. This influences the way in which new tasks are handled.

No previous mention has been made of the need for attention. Because so much information is constantly wanting our attention, there is in us some mechanism which helps us to attend to certain events rather than others. It is a mechanism which integrates our perceptual process. The example of driving a car is often given to illustrate the process of attention and its attendant integration. The teacher has to stimulate pupils to attend, since this will provide for integration, and this is an important component of lesson planning. As a student respondent wrote:

In order to achieve motivation in the class: (a) I try to involve students in the learning — make them give their own opinions/write their own appreciations (of poems) for the class (arousal), and encourage brainstorming on other occasions (ie What feelings does the poet express in this poem?); (b) I try to give them more confidence, raise their goals. Reduce 'bias' by presenting material in a 'presentable' manner (expectancy); (c) I establish a happy but business-like environment in the class (discipline); (d) I praise the students who are showing signs of improvement, etc.

In so far as the other stages are concerned, these depend very much on the learning strategies employed in the classroom. (These are the subject of the next two chapters.) Finally, we return to one of the key aims of this chapter, namely the relationship between pupil and instructor and to an effect known as cognitive dissonance.

When a subject is cognitively complex and where values are involved, such as in political studies, a pupil may be in disagreement with the views held by the teacher. In these circumstances there may be considerable resistance to learning, and apparently this is particularly likely to be the case if the students are only mildly critical of the teacher's standpoint. Such students may become alienated from the political and economic system. However, as Marshall (1980) shows, a teacher can cause learning through his teaching style, even if his or her rating with the students deteriorates during the course.

Remembering that we impose meaning on the objects of knowledge it should come as no surprise to find that a pupil can deliberately impose misunderstanding in order to achieve consistency between the message and his feelings. If there is inconsistency, a pupil can change his attitude to a teacher from like to dislike if the teacher's messages appear to be untenable. This can happen in university when first-year students have to cope with certain value propositions in the social and behavioural sciences: anything that is the opposite of student views can create such dissonance. As a Catholic, I found the study of some aspects of sociology most difficult for this reason.

More generally, Eggleston (1977) suggests:

There are many examples of dissonance in the curriculum. In the expressive subjects such as art and music, teachers are commonly concerned with 'helping children to express themselves' in such matters as music, dress, leisure and so on. Yet they are regularly heard to complain that students 'reject' the expressive activities they offer both out of school and after school. But it is not that the children are uninvolved in music, dress or leisure, rather that they have alternative perceptions of these matters that are either unrelated to or opposed to those of the teachers. It is important to remember that this does not mean that children are unable to respond to the teacher's construction of reality in these matters; indeed, most children quickly learn to perform in school in the ways approved by the teacher. Many writers have reminded us that what the child learns above all is how to give an acceptable performance.

This example provides yet another instance of the influence of the hidden curriculum in the classroom.

Some notes on research on pupil behaviour in the classroom

A useful introduction to this subject is to be found in Chapter 7 of Turner, 1977 (see below for references). Special reference to Nash's study (1973) has been made above (pp 67-9). A further note on Kelly's theory of personality and the repertory grid technique which Nash used is given below.

Investigations of this kind are concerned with the problem of objectivity. Early investigations studied the climate of the classroom. One study used recordings of teachers in classrooms: these were analysed into seven categories and from them pictures of the socio-emotional climate of the classroom were developed. Subsequently, attempts were made to relate teacher behaviour to classroom climate.

The complexity of the problem yielded numerous categories. Nash used Kelly's repertory grid technique to resolve this problem. In 1955 G A Kelly published a theory of personality. A simple introduction to this theory is given by Bannister (1966). In addition to describing the theory, often called personal construct theory, a method for testing the theory – the repertory grid technique – was put forward. The technique has attracted much interest among researchers, and has been used by this writer in the analysis of jobs of professional people (Youngman et al, 1978).

Kelly's theory begins with the notion that man is a scientist, and that his life consists of a series of predictions which are tested. A person views the world with a map, made up of bi-polar constructs as for example like compared with dislike. To find out what a person's disposition is, one must find out what his or her constructs are. The repertory grid is a technique for eliciting these constructs. Nash found the six constructs most used by teachers in primary and secondary schools to be:

1. Keeps order/is unable to keep order
2. Teaches you/does not teach you
3. Explains/does not explain
4. Interesting/boring
5. Fair/unfair
6. Friendly/unfriendly.

Turner draws particular attention to a study by Kousin (1970) which looks at the behavioural categories in a successful classroom, defined as one 'having a high prevalence of work involvement and low measure of misbehaviour in learning settings'.

There has been much interest in inter-action analysis, a technique developed by Flanders and elaborated by Amidon and Hough. When Flanders began his work previous research had led him to the view that it did not answer the question, 'Why and when should a teacher react in either a dominative or integrative manner?' To put it in another way, 'Why and when should a teacher give orders or praise and encourage?' To obtain information which would lead to an understanding of the ways in which short term behaviour patterns influenced momentary decisions and which would take into account the degree of flexibility in a teacher's behaviour, he devised a technique (which amounts to a checklist for the observation of teacher-pupil inter-actions). The categories were constructed around three main parameters: (i) teacher talk – indirect influence, (ii) teacher talk – direct influence, and (iii) student talk.

Direct influence consists of stating the teacher's own opinion or ideas, directing the pupil's action, criticizing his behaviour, or justifying the teacher's authority or use of that authority. Indirect influence consists of soliciting the opinions or ideas of the pupils, applying or enlarging on those opinions or ideas, praising or encouraging the participation of pupils, or clarifying and accepting their feelings. (Flanders *in* Amidon and Hough)

These categories can be developed into smaller ones, and the whole makes up a schedule which can be used to code teaching-learning activities.

As a training device, this technique may sharpen the perception of a student teacher. However, an objection to the technique is that the schedule may cloud the perception of the observer: it predetermines what the observer looks at. This objection was taken up by Delamont (Stubbs and Delamont, 1976), who considered that the anthropological approach of participant observation should be made to such studies. To participate as a learner would ensure that all significant events were noted. Other research showed that classrooms have a personality which is the construct of the teachers in their inter-action with their pupils. (This writer has conducted a participant observation study among students in a university class, which is written up jointly in Heywood and Montagu-Pollock (1976).

References

M L J Abercrombie (1960) *The Anatomy of Judgement. An Investigation into the Processes of Perception and Reasoning.* Harmondsworth: Penguin.

T W Adorno, E Frenkel-Brunswick, D J Levinson and R N Sanford (1950) *The Authoritarian Personality.* New York: Harper and Row.

M Ainscow and D A Tweddle (1979) *Preventing Classroom Failure: An Objectives Approach.* London: Wiley.

E J Amidon and J B Hough (1967) *Interaction Analysis: Theory, Research and Application.* Reading, Mass: Addison-Wesley.

G W Allport (1961) *Pattern and Growth in Personality.* New York: Holt, Rinehart and Winston.

D Bannister (1966) *in* B Foss (ed) *New Horizons in Psychology*, Vol 1. Harmondsworth: Penguin.

S J Cattling (1979) Maps and cognitive maps: the young child's perception, *Geography*, November, 299.

G H Early (1969) *Perceptual Training in the Curriculum.* Columbus, Ohio: Charles Merrill.

J Eggleston (1977) *The Sociology of the School Curriculum.* London: Routledge and Kegan Paul.

P Hesseling (1966) *Strategy of Evaluation Research.* Aassen: Van Gorcum.

J Heywood and H Montagu-Pollock (1976) *Science for Arts Students: A Case Study in Curriculum Development.* Guildford, Surrey: Society for Research into Higher Education.

L Hudson (1966) *Contrary Imaginations.* London: Methuen.

N C Kephart (1960) *The Slow Learner in the Classroom.* Columbus, Ohio: Charles Merrill.

J S Kousin (1970) *Discipline and Group Management in Classrooms.* New York: Holt, Rinehart and Winston.

S Marshall (1980) Cognitive-affective dissonance in the classroom, *Teaching Political Science*, 8, 111-17.

R Nash (1973) *Classrooms Observed.* London: Methuen.

E Roach and N C Kephart (1966) *The Purdue Perceptual-Motor Survey.* Columbus, Ohio: Charles Merrill.

M Rokeach (1960) *The Open and Closed Mind.* New York: Basic Books.

Rules and Programmes for the Intermediate and Leaving Certificate Examinations. Dublin: Government Publications (published annually).

F Slater (1976) The concept of perception and the geography teacher, *McGill Journal of Education*, 11 (2), 166.

M Stubbs and S Delamont (eds) (1976) *Explorations in Classroom Management.* London: Wiley.

J Turner (1977) *Psychology for the Classroom*. London: Methuen.

D Uzzell (1976) Children's perception and understanding of their environment, *BEE*, October, 11.

G M Weinberg (1976) *An Introduction to General Systems Thinking*. New York: Wiley.

H F Woodhouse (1979) Ambiguity: some implications and consequences, *Studies*, 265-76.

M B Youngman, R Oxtoby, J D Monk and J Heywood (1978) *Analysing Jobs*. Farnborough: Gower Press.

References for the Nottingham University School of Education Teacher Education Project

 (i) A Flanders type schedule can be found in:
   P Dooley (ed) *Nottingham Class Management Observation Schedule* (trial materials).

 (ii) Involving teachers and fellow students:
   J A Partington *Observing Modern Language Teaching — A Workbook* (Focus 2A). *Observing Science Teaching* (Focus 2B) (trial materials).

(iii) Involving fellow student rating schedules of own work:
   T Kerry *Effective Questioning* (Focus F) (trial materials).
   K Selkirk *Teaching Mathematics* (Focus 2C) (trial materials).

5 Concepts and Cognitive Development

5.1 Organizing questions

(a) Organizing questions embracing the next three chapters

1. 'Education is necessarily an eclectic subject.' Discuss this statement with reference to the contrasting theories of instruction of Bruner, Gagné and Ausubel and their application to your work in the classroom.

2. What implications do the findings of educational research in the field of learning have for the teacher? Illustrate your answer by reference to the subject you teach.

3. With reference to the subject you teach describe Gagné's approach to the sequencing of learning skills.

4. 'Every instructor and every school should formulate defensible theories of learning and instruction.' With reference to your own teaching activities describe and defend your own theories of learning and instruction showing in particular how they influence the strategies you use in the classroom in regard to pupil attitudes and pupil performance.

5. How applicable are learning principles and learning theories to a theory of instruction? Describe any one method of instruction which is based on clearly stated learning axioms.

(b) Relating to this chapter

1. What are the implications of educational research on concept learning for the timing and planning of lessons? Illustrate your answer with reference to your own work.

2. 'The issue is not learning from textbooks and learning from "real-life" experiences. We do not know as yet what experiences are likely to facilitate learning of many concepts. The teacher will undoubtedly use a variety of experiences, but the whole experience must be simplified so that the essential characteristics of a concept can be determined easily by the child' (McDonald). Why is it that many real life introductions to concepts are not very successful in learning? Give examples of 'real' concepts which might confuse,

and simplifed examples which might enhance learning from the work you have done in your own subject.

3. Distinguish between concept and principle. How, in your opinion, should the findings of educational research influence instructional strategies for teaching concepts? Illustrate your answer by reference to the subject you teach.

4. Carpenter in his study of the way in which concepts are formed concluded: 'This study suggests that together with what is already known, the teacher may find profit in: (1) being certain that the desired response is performed before assuming that learning has occurred (far too often teachers seem to operate on the assumption of osmosis and that this absorption of knowledge will guarantee sufficient transfer to the level of application); (2) noting the various responses that compose a skill, act, or complex behaviour, and making sure that ample reinforcement is contiguous with them instead of rewarding only end results. This suggests that we focus attention upon the behavioural processes instead of only products.' What does Carpenter mean by process and product in this context? Illustrate your answer by reference to the subject you teach and indicate how this view should influence patterns of assessment and examining.

5. Discuss the use of examples and non-examples in teaching your own subject. In what ways would you allow research in this area to influence the teaching strategies you adopt?

6. How would you advise a trainee teacher to approach the teaching of concepts and on what basis would that advice be given? Illustrate your answer by reference to the subject you teach.

7. 'We may frequently test for behaviour not likely to be retained.' Describe an experiment which illustrates this point and show by example the relevance of the teaching technique used to your own subject.

5.2 Organizing language: the term 'concept' and its uses

The primary aim of this chapter is to discuss how concepts such as 'harbour', 'mountain', 'particle', 'poverty' are best taught. How do pupils best learn such concepts? What is the relative importance of the concepts in the subject you teach? Often, teachers spend more time on teaching relatively minor concepts than on those which matter. It is also important to think about the difference between factual information (knowledge) and concepts. Again, teachers often spend more time on giving factual information which can be learned through independent study than on ensuring that pupils can understand the concepts that are fundamental to their subject. Without such understanding there can be no independent transfer of learning (expansion of knowledge).

The term concept is also used in the sense of conceptualization, a capability to solve abstract problems. Piaget's stage theory of intellectual development distinguishes between levels of conceptualization appropriate to a given age-span or entering characteristics. Clearly some concepts are more abstract than others. A highly intelligent person is sometimes described as one who is capable of a high level of abstract thought. Associated with these different levels of abstraction are different kinds of skill and interpretation. Lonergan's study of method in history will be used to exemplify this point.

The chapter begins with two examples to reinforce the ideas of perception and entering characteristics discussed in the previous chapters. As an example of motivation (the relationship between interest and enacted performance) Whitehead's rhythmic or stage theory of learning is introduced. Sections 5.5 and 5.6 are devoted to the ideas of Bruner, Lonergan and Piaget. Section 5.7 is devoted to concept learning, and begins with a categorization of human capabilities with the intention of distinguishing, first, between concepts, principles and problem solving, and second, between a theory of learning and a theory of instruction.

5.3 Perception and entering characteristics

What appears clear and straightforward to the teacher (as in the instructions I gave for a class test) may appear such to a small number of his pupils, but there remain a substantial number confused, because everybody perceives concepts in different ways. This difference in perception (as research tells us) is due to a large extent to the differences in concept structure in the children entering school, which in turn is due to the previous experience of the child and the environment in which he lives.

The first step in order to answer this question is to define a concept. 'A concept is a class of stimuli which have common characteristics.' It is further broken into attributes and values which are of the utmost importance for consideration by the teacher before he considers planning his lessons.

In order to time and plan his lesson effectively in relation to concept learning the teacher must determine the entering behaviour of the student. Has the student acquired the prerequisite understanding? What experience either first or second hand has the pupil had to date which will influence the learning situation? Certainly negative transfer of learning will impinge on the situation — an example from my own experience which comes to mind is of a pupil in my second-year English class who was a native Irish speaker having been reared in a totally Irish environment until her thirteenth year. Her constant procedure to convey her thought in Irish directly into English had a bad effect on her English essay writing. I, however, being unacquainted with the entering behaviour of the student until six weeks had elapsed, am an example of a teacher who had not correctly assessed the importance of timing and planning in teaching particular concepts to my pupils.

These illustrations show the importance of perception and entering characteristics on subsequent performance. By implication they illustrate the relevance of motivation in learning. As another student wrote, the best time for concept learning is during the first 20 minutes when the students' attention has been aroused.

5.4 Abstraction and conceptualization: some student responses

The pupils in fourth class are mainly in the concrete operations stage in intellectual development according to Piaget's theory. As such, concepts had to be made very real. Diagrams, pictures, postcards, etc were collected of various concepts like 'harbour'. A large collection of material was therefore on hand in explaining the concept 'harbour'. The important elements were then discussed until the important elements of what made up a harbour were listed and understood. The children were then able to understand the concept.

Piaget in his theory advocates the fact that cognitive growth is continuous, yet one can distinguish the cognitive stages which he defines as being periods of temporary stability. This is his theory of auto-regulation or equilibration. He claims that we have been through a succession of disequilibria which are caused by ontogenetic change which can occur from within or from the environmental input. As children do not like disequilibria they must accommodate this by adjusting their previous knowledge accordingly. This is important to consider when one is planning a class: it is vitally important that the concepts involved in a class are within the capabilities of the class.

Bruner traces three stages of concept learning. The first is enactive, where the child is manipulating physical objects. The second is ikonic, where the child is manipulating the words. The final stage is the symbolic, where the child is able to manipulate concepts. By following this progression, the child is involved in concept learning.

Bruner, being a rationalist, feels that ideas are, in their essence, simple. It is invariably the presentation which is complex. I am in full agreement with Bruner here. I have often gone into the classroom knowing my material and lesson-plan and fully aware that the lesson was single. Only in the classroom did I then realize that the idea was simple, but my presentation was far too complex.

In order to develop a concept a student must have the ability to both discriminate (amongst different objects) and generalize (amongst different objects with similar characteristics). A teacher, therefore, is under the obligation to ensure that each pupil is given the opportunity to make valid and accurate perceptions of the concept being studied. In order to ensure that this occurs it is worthwhile to introduce each concept in three stages — the enactive, the ikonic and the symbolic.

These three stages represent roughly the developmental stages described by psychologists such as Piaget and it would appear that allowing a pupil to progress through them gives him a firm foundation and accurate understanding of most concepts. This is illustrated in G H Early's experiment with the styrofoam ball/globe. The pupils first went through the enactive stage where they cut the concentric circles and made a sphere from them. This was then covered with papier mâché. They had witnessed and experienced the coming together of a whole from the parts. They then proceeded to the ikonic stage in which using a torch they located the north pole on their 'globe'. Finally, in the symbolic stage they were allowed to hypothesize as to how the south pole could be located.

A subject can be taught in a way suitable to the child's intellectual development. For example, in geography the complex concept of weather instability could be taught in an enactive way by having the children measure rainfall, temperature, wind speed, etc themselves, rather than in an ikonic way, using diagrams, or a symbolic way, just talking about it and hypothesizing.

5.5 Theories of cognitive development

(a) Piaget's theory

Piaget, to whom the first respondents refer, has made a major contribution to the theories of psychological development. Although he said that it had no direct bearing on instructional practice, it has in fact had a profound influence on educational practice, especially in the primary school.

Piaget objected to the traditional view of maturation, which noted that there were orderly biological changes from birth, through adolescence to adulthood and that such development was unlearned and instinctual. Nevertheless, the idea that cognitive development takes place in stages is a maturational idea, but it is associated with the concept of 'readiness to learn'. This has been related by many teachers and investigators to reading.

The theory of psychological development presented by Piaget contains four elements, the first three of which are to be found in other theories. They are:

1. biological maturation;
2. experience with the physical environment;
3. experience with the social environment;
4. equilibration.

In regard to the experience of the physical environment Piaget suggested that in addition to exercise and physical experience (which relate to the development of the sensorimotor skills — see Chapter 8 — and the ways in which we learn to extract information from the objects in the environment), there is a *logico-mathematical experience* which depends on the way in which the subject and its object interact. Piaget takes a Platonic position and argues that within the mind there is (Hilgard and Bower, 1975) 'a cognitive "know-how" which Piaget calls *structure*'.

In order to count, a person has to abstract all the qualities from an object (eg colour, shape) in order to use the object as a 'counter'. Piaget argues that this is a difficult logical operation. The child can learn to impose order on objects. Given a straight line of objects the child can establish that the same number are present when counted from the right or from the left. The fact that a child can do that is of considerable importance. The fact that the child can also rearrange the objects illustrates that it not only experiences the physical environment but contributes to that environment.

Much interest has been focused on this theory by those concerned with the development of the new mathematics. They have argued that the structures of new mathematics relate to the logico-mathematical structures of the mind. If this is the case then children should obtain a better mathematical understanding from study through the conceptual structure provided by the new mathematics curriculum. Needless to say such arguments are controversial.

In regard to the social environment, Piaget assigns most importance to language since it is the basis of our experience of socialization. However, he argues that the development of logical operations is prior to that of language. This is consistent with his concept of logico-mathematical structures and the notion that there are in-built structures in the mind which have to be brought out. Language aids this development: it is a servant of the intelligence which evolves in stages.

The fourth stage — equilibration — co-ordinates the influences of the other three factors. It is a process which may be understood by reference to the theory of perceptual learning presented in the preceding chapter. Piaget suggests there are *schemes* or *structures* which enable the child to *assimilate* the external environment. But the *assimilation* of new information also requires that there should be a change in the existing structures so that there is congruence between external reality and the child's mental structures. This process is called *accommodation*. *Equilibration* is the adjustive process required for assimilation and accommodation.

An interesting feature of Piaget's theory is the attempt to relate it to the epistemological processes which go on in the child's mind as it learns by solving problems. Piaget's often quoted example is of the way a child uses clay. From experimenting with clay rolled into a sausage shape, it learns that:

1. there is less clay in a thin sausage and more in a long sausage;

2. a sausage can be long and thin;
3. a sausage can become longer and thinner;
4. if a sausage can become longer, it can become shorter;
5. length and thickness can compensate for each other.

The transition between 2 (configuration) and 3 (transformation) is an example of equilibration: the child learns by his actions on its environment. Level 5 is called *conservation* by Piaget because a transformation does not change the quantity of matter.

Textbooks often illustrate this point with an illustration of two beakers of different diameter. Each has the same volume of water, but the level of the water is different in each. At first a child may think there is more water in the beaker with the smaller diameter since it is at a higher level. Several deductions have to be made to arrive at the conclusion that there is the same amount of water in both beakers.

Piaget argues that children move through orderly stages of development. The first stage is from birth to about one-and-a-half years. This is the development of sensorimotor intelligence, closely related to the perceptual motor development discussed in the last chapter. Within this stage, there are six sub-stages. Each of these is a problem-solving activity involving its own logic. Thus after about 18 months the child is able to solve a detour problem by going round a barrier even if this means departing from the original goal for a short time. The child can infer causes from the observation of effects, and begins to predict effects from observing causes; the child also begins to invent applications of something previously learned.

The second major stage of development is called the period of representative intelligence and concrete operations. This takes up to 11 or 12 years. The first part of this period is between two and seven years and is called the pre-operational phase. The second phase is that of concrete operations. It is in this period that the child learns *conservation*. For example, the size-weight illusion described above is resolved. Children tackle this problem in relation to matter, weight and volume. Piaget claims that the order of such learning is invariable. Learning by doing is the essence of concrete operations. In this period children learn to seriate, classify and establish correspondence.

The final period when the child moves from middle childhood to adolescence is that of formal operations. Now the child is able to undertake abstract thinking, to hypothesize and deduct, experiment and theorize. It is the stage of in-built maturity.

This summary does less than justice to the descriptive material offered by Piaget and his supporters to support their view that intellectual development takes place in invariable stages. Its attraction to teachers will be obvious since the experiments (observations) which led to the theory provide teaching materials appropriate to the supposed level of development in the child. Moreover, it is easy (rightly or wrongly), as the student responses illustrate, for teachers to make judgements about children in terms of these stages. They see that a child cannot handle certain concepts in their own subject and may wrongly conclude that the child is at the stage of concrete operations.

Piaget's experimental approach has been criticized. The idea that children are not capable of philosophical puzzlement early in their lives has been challenged by G B Matthews (1980) in a book which ought to be compulsory reading for student teachers. Nevertheless it is a common observation of teachers that there is a sequence in the child's development towards the understanding of conservation. Teachers have shown how Piaget's theory can contribute to the development of teaching programmes in the secondary school as, for example, Shayer's work on the science curriculum (1980).

Some of Piaget's notions are of immense significance to the teacher. First is the idea that we learn by doing, which suggests there is likely to be some value in discovery learning (see Chapter 6). Despite the Western philosophical tradition and its influence on university education, there is much to suggest that we arrive at theories as a result of the need to solve practical problems (MacMurray, 1957). Arising from this it is clear that the concrete illustration is often necessary if we are to understand an abstraction. This suggests that we solve problems through stages similar to those marked out by Piaget for long period development. It also seems evident that some people never arrive at the level of formal operations. We learn from the respondents that individual pupils within the same class perform at different levels if different kinds of teaching are used. Developmental theories of intelligence force us to consider where a person is and how modifiable he is at that time. At the very minimum Piaget provides us with important insights into the way in which individuals learn.

(b) Bruner's theory

Jerome Bruner offered an alternative cognitive-developmental theory of learning and instruction to Piaget's in *The Process of Education* (1960) and subsequent publications. The three features of his writings which are of special interest to student teachers relate to the teaching of advanced concepts, the sequence of development, and the need to account for the ways in which children actually solve problems. He more than anyone else fostered the practice of discovery learning in the school curriculum, an idea also found in the work of John Dewey (1930) and strongly supported by Piaget. But Bruner differs from Piaget in that he believes learning situations should be structured to enable the child to learn on its own.

Bruner outlines four characteristics of a theory of instruction. These are:

1. *Predisposition to learn.* A theory of instruction must be concerned with the experiences and contexts that will tend to make the child willing and able to learn when he enters school.
2. *Structure of knowledge.* A theory of instruction must specify ways in which a body of knowledge should be structured so that it can

be most readily grasped by the learner.
3. *Sequence.* A theory of instruction should specify the most effective sequences in which to present the materials.
4. *Reinforcement.* A theory of instruction should specify the nature and pacing of rewards, moving from extrinsic rewards to intrinsic ones. (Bruner, 1966)

These have to take into account individual differences as well as the differences between the structure of knowledge in different fields. Bruner argued in 1960 that 'Any subject can be taught effectively in some intellectually honest form to any child at any stage of development', a position which is markedly different from that of Piaget. I attempted to demonstrate this idea (1960) through the publication of a work on Einstein's scientific contribution aimed at the 12-year-old. It does not imply that a child will be able to do exercises in the theory of relativity, but my view is akin to that of Whitehead, who suggested that learning took place in three stages: romance, grammar and generalization. Romance is a stage of curiosity: it is not a stage of analysis. We need a stage of romance to stimulate interest.

In Bruner's theory of cognitive development the three modes of representation follow in sequence. The first is called *enactive*. Bruner notes that conditioning and stimulus-response learning are appropriate to this mode: it is learning through action without words. The second stage, which is one of mental representation, is called *ikonic* (taken from the word *icon*). In this stage the child uses concrete visual imagery. It may be related to Gestalt psychology. The final stage of representation is the *symbolic*. Because children are able to translate experience into language and think with language, they are able to develop abstract images. Bruner holds the belief that children can be helped to learn at the level of most advanced kind of thinking in which they engage. That is, a teacher can help a child develop more sophisticated kinds of thought process. Thus Bruner would argue that we should *teach* readiness; we do not have to wait for it. In contrast, Piaget believes that children have to develop at their own pace and should not be subject to training for higher levels of thought.

5.6 Subject methodologies and structure

In Exhibit 5.1 I have set out my interpretation of the relationship between Whitehead, Bruner and Piaget's theories of learning. To these I have added Lonergan's analysis of method in history since it is a stage theory which is clearly related to different levels of abstraction.

Whitehead's is a slightly different but nevertheless related theory. He identifies three stages in learning. The first is a stage of romance. This is a stage of first apprehension. The subject matter has the vividness of novelty; it holds within itself unexplained connections with possibilities half-disclosed by glimpses and half-concealed by a wealth of material. In this

PIAGET	WHITEHEAD	LONERGAN	BRUNER	LONERGAN
Stages of mental growth (implied)	*Stages of mental growth*	*Understanding and knowing*	*Theory of instruction (method)*	*Experiencing and knowing*
Pre-formal operations	Romance	Pre-critical history Artistic Ethical Explanatory Apologetic Prophetic	Specify experiences which most effectively implant in an individual a predisposition to learning	Autobiography
Concrete operations	Precision	Critical history Heuristic Ecstatic Selective Critical Constructive	Specify ways in which the body of knowledge should be structured so that it can be readily grasped by the learner	Biography
Formal operations	Generalization	Second level critical history (professional)	Specify the most effective sequences in which to present the material to be learned	Historiography
			Specify the nature and pacing of rewards and punishments in the process of learning and teaching (ie evaluation)	

Exhibit 5.1 *Theories of cognitive development compared* (Heywood, 1974)

stage knowledge is not dominated by systematic procedure. The second stage is of precision. This is the stage of 'growing into the apprehension of principles by the acquisition of precise knowledge of details', and emerging from the comparative passivity of being trained into the active freedom of appreciation. Precise knowledge will grow more actively than before, because the mind has experienced the power of definiteness and responds to the acquisition of general truth and illustration. The growth of knowledge becomes progressively unconscious, being derived from some active adventure of thought. Whitehead's third stage is that of generalization, in which new romance and precision are brought together in new syntheses.

The relationship between these stages and those of primary, secondary and tertiary education would seem to be self-evident. But isn't our approach to learning any new subject similar? We need the romance before the precision, and the precision before the generalization. There is also a fairly clear relationship with the stage ideas of Piaget, modified by the view that all learning begins with the solution to practical concrete problems.

Similarities between Lonergan's view of method in history and these theories are also apparent. Lonergan (1971) writes of pre-critical history as follows:

> Its vehicle is narrative, an ordered recital of events. It recounts who did what, when, where, under what circumstances, from what motives, with what results. Its function is practical . . . it is never just a narrative of bald facts. It is *artistic*: it selects, orders, describes . . . It is *ethical*: it not only narrates, but also apportions praise and blame. It is *explanatory*: it accounts for existing institutions by telling of their origins and development and by contrasting them with alternative institutions found in other lands. It is *apologetic*: correcting false or tendentious accounts of the people's past, and refuting the calumnies of neighbouring peoples . . . It is *prophetic*: to hindsight about the past there is joined foresight on the future and there are added the recommendations of a man of wide reading and modest wisdom.

Inspection of this list shows that pre-critical history is achieved by the adoption of a certain behaviour pattern composed of a number of well defined skills, which are the second order objectives. Pre-critical history is a problem-solving process based on the narrative method, and it lends itself to the stage of romance in mental growth since romance gives the student a predisposition toward the learning of history. It is a stage of motivation. Method, or better still, the type of learning experience is all important to success at this stage. To grasp the role of history in understanding the social and cultural process, one may possibly begin with existential history, that is with oneself. Through autobiography and biography, a student can be shown the problem of self-evaluation, the problem of the third person and personal beliefs, the problem of fragmentary data and the problem of uncertainty.

However, the stage of precision in learning history demands a more critical approach. Its second order objectives are, according to my interpretation of Lonergan:

1. *Heuristic:* the bringing to light of relevant data.
2. *Ecstatic (imaginative):* the leading of the inquirer out of his original perspectives and into perspectives proper to his object.
3. *Selective:* selecting from the totality of data those relevant to the understanding achieved.
4. *Critical:* removing from one use or context to another the data that might otherwise be thought relevant to present tasks.
5. *Constructive (synthesis):* data are selected and knotted together by the vast and intricate web of interconnecting links that cumulatively come to light as understanding progresses.

Clearly, the first four of these objectives belong to the stage of precision. The pupil must apply the biographical method to the community: he proceeds from the data made available by research, through imaginative reconstruction and cumulative questioning and answering towards related sets of concepts so that he sees a developing and/or deteriorating unity constituted by co-operations, by institutions, by personal relations, by a functioning and/or malfunctioning of order, by a communal realization of originating and terminal values and disvalues.

The implications of such theories for both method and syllabus in the different subjects of the curriculum are considerable. But our concern here is primarily with the teaching of concepts within the secondary curriculum. This particular discussion must be regarded as advanced organization for further study.

5.7 Teaching and learning concepts

(a) The significance of concepts in learning

The examples given below in the advanced organizers assume a definition of 'concept'. Since they are about the teaching and learning of concepts, it is useful to begin this section with a definition of the word.

The textbooks tell us that a concept is 'a classification of stimuli which have common characteristics'. In the advanced organizers we find these concepts: pulse, poverty, waltz, adverb, adjective, particle, solid and liquid. These range from the simple to the complex, from the apparently concrete to the abstract. Some are more precise than others, and are essential to a subject's understanding. Without them the world would remain complex. We acquire concepts all the time, for they enable us to interpret our experience of the world: they make generalizations and instruction possible, and reduce the necessity for constant learning.

In his early work on *The Conditions of Learning* (1976), Gagné distinguished eight levels of complexity in learning:

1. Signal learning
2. Stimulus response learning
3. S-R chains
4. Verbal associations
5. Discriminations
6. Concepts
7. Rules (principles)
8. Problem solving.

The significance of concepts is shown by their position at level 6. Concept formation is a high level of mental processing, hence its importance to the teacher. Gagné argues that each level requires the preceding type as a prerequisite of learning at that level.

(b) Organizing responses on the teaching and learning of concepts

1. This approach to concept formation has been verified in my classroom with reference to the teaching of the concept of *pulse* (as mentioned earlier). It is a fundamental concept vital to an understanding of rhythmic features and characteristics in music.

   Initially, I invited the children to feel their pulses, as a prelude to the conjuration of the mental image of a constantly throbbing beat. The dominant attributes of the concept were stressed, ie regularity, compactness and underlying strength. (Of course, the terminology presented to 13- and 14-year-olds was much simpler than that used above.) Examples — mostly positive — were given of various rhythmic patterns. The pupils were asked to identify the pulse. Finally, it was realized that frequent reference to the attributes and characteristics of 'pulse' strengthened the retention and recall of the pupils when the concept was reintroduced and revised at regular, frequent intervals.

2. The concept which I was trying to get across to the children was poverty. What is it? Where is it? How does it affect us?

   It was useful to see what de Cecco and Crawford had to say about it and their example of how to present the concept of tourist was helpful. There are seven basic steps according to them in presenting a topic. First of all one needs to describe what the task is. Secondly one needs to analyse what will be needed to get this across. These two steps are done very much by me before the course begins. I went through many items which I thought might be useful. The third step for me was the one when I brought the class into action. This gave the class some 'hooks' to hang their ideas of poverty on. They wrote a paragraph on what they believed poverty was.

   The fourth step involved presenting positive and negative ideas of the concepts. This was done through reading a passage from a book entitled *Rich Christians in an Age of Hunger* which presented very vividly the two sides of poverty. We also played a game which put the children in the place of the poor and how they would react. The fifth step that de Cecco and Crawford advocate is the presentation of examples together one after another. This was done in the form of a slide show presented by one of the Third World relief organizations. The sixth step of allowing student response was by turning the blackboard into a graffiti board and the children wrote their responses to what they felt poverty was and our attitude to it was. The final stage of assessing how much they learned was never accomplished due to school exams.

3. The waltz is a conjunctive concept with several attributes and values added together. I decided that the most important distinguishing characteristics to be presented to the class were the following:

    1. *tune:* the number and kind of beats in each bar.
    2. *rhythm:* the characteristic note values.
    3. *tempo:* the speed of the beat.

In a waltz: 1: 3/4
            2: crotchet
            3: lively

The occasion, social milieu and national temperament are also important because they did dictate the type of dance but they were not as distinguishing as the main three attributes.

I was thus ready to begin my class. At the beginning, I told them 'at the end of this class, when you have been presented with various examples of dance music, you will be able to determine those examples which are explained by the concept waltz'.

Useful verbal mediators obviously included tune, rhythm and tempo and I made sure that they understood these ideas before moving on further.

Positive examples:
Waltzes of: Johann Strauss Senior
             Johann Strauss Junior
             Waldteufel
             Gung'l
             Lanner
             Lehar and if necessary other Viennese
             waltz composers

Negative examples:
Pavan: a stately court dance in 4/4 time
Polonaise
Mazurka

I needed to take care here to include only examples that the children might appreciate. There would be no use including examples of Czardas (Hungarian folk-dances) or Trepaho (Russian folk-dances) to assess the concept.

One interesting fact I did point out was that the waltz was frowned on by the establishment. For example, Heinrich Laube once said: 'African, hot-blooded, crazy with life . . . restless, unbeautiful, passionate . . . he exorcises the witched devils from our body (Strauss Senior) . . .' etc. This is of course explained by the big discrepancy between what actually happened: the result was shock and abhorrence. I left the class with the remark that the punk movement could well be explained in like manner which immediately provoked discussion.

4. As an English teacher I would have to teach the concept of adverb or adjective after that of noun or verb; of metaphor after simile and so on. I would do a brief task analysis, isolating prerequisite concepts. For an adverb I would have to focus on the descriptive aspect; the '-ly' ending (suppressing, for the moment until a later stage, irregular adverbs, and the principle of '-y' ending adjectives as interference at this stage). Question and answer would elicit the degree of familiarity with prerequisite concepts (noun, adjective, and so on). I would then state the objective (you will recognize adverbs — describing action words — and illustrate them). I would evoke prerequisite concepts and oral use of adverb. (As so often in language teaching, the child 'knows' it — but I am discriminating it; generalizing it as a class; and denoting it usually for future recognition 'as' an adverb.) I would then list a series of adverbs, in sentence form, to aid meaningful recognition, colouring the adverb brightly and differently. I would then just point to adverbs and non-adverbs for recognition, and then I would list a series of words for a similar question and answer approach, gradually distinguishing other words ending in '-ly' (eg lively) or just '-y' (eg snowy) from adverbs; all examples remain on the board to aid retention and allow random reinforcement. I would conclude by following discrimination practice (done by pupils themselves) to generalization — confirmation — the children would recognize new adverbs.

5. One must remember that in language teaching one must not teach a concept in the second language if the student has not mastered his understanding of the concepts in the first language. However if classifications can be made in one language they can obviously be applied in a second language situation.

6. An experiment which has been done is:
Three groups:

Group A	Group B	Group G
Two simple concepts	One simple concept	None
Complex concept learned best	Second best	Third

I did this in my two classes. One class learned the concept of the particle theory of matter and later learned the concepts of solids, liquids and gases. The second class learned the concepts of solid, liquids and gases without the first concept being learned. In a test I gave each class, the first class showed a much better understanding of the second concepts.

7. Very often we as teachers can take for granted that the children have certain concepts which we regard as elementary. I was teaching eight-year-olds various characteristics of animals after a visit to the zoo. I was using the concept 'desert' very easily and freely only to discover later on in the lesson that at least two children had thought a 'desert' was another animal. I had failed to teach the concept desert adequately before using it as a generalization. So we must teach concepts to children by pointing out the essential characteristics.

(c) Commentary

The first two responses refer to a theory of instruction teaching for concepts. This theory begins with the definition of the concept, that it is a class of stimuli having common characteristics. From this definition we may infer that a person requires cognitive skills in discrimination and generalization. First of all we have to be able to discriminate one concept from another. This means that we have to establish the common characteristics of each concept. With the aid of these characteristics we are then able to generalize. The teacher's role is clear: it is to enable the child to develop these skills with the aid of the concepts used in the subject taught. To put it another way, the teacher has to relate these concepts to the pupil's experience in a meaningful way.

To assist the pupils with discrimination, teachers will find it of use to distinguish between concept attributes, attribute values and the way in which some attributes dominate others.

Concepts will normally have more than one attribute. The square blocks which make up a Rubik Cube have both colour and form. The form is that of a cube. Both the colour and the form are major attributes, for the object of the Rubik exercise is to produce a large cube in which all the smaller cubes form six surfaces each of a different colour. There will be minor attributes, and these sometimes dominate a person's thinking and are the cause of misunderstanding. However, dominant concepts will have dominant attributes: concept learning is most difficult when the attributes are not obvious. A teacher has therefore to ensure that the children comprehend the major attributes. Part of the skill of discrimination is to recognize that while an attribute is a distinctive feature of a concept it varies from concept to concept. The way in which a child acquires information from modelling clay (see section 5.5) is an example of how the application of such attributes as size and volume (which are themselves concepts) are learned. The number of attributes will vary between concepts.

Associated with any attribute will be a value. For example, the colour of a peach will vary from yellow to crimson. A yellow peach may not be distinguishable from a yellow golden delicious apple at a distance. But on a greengrocer's stand, they will be readily distinguished because other concepts relating to the characteristics of the skin will be used to make the distinction. The changes in colour of the peach are changes in value.

Learning is also helped if the teacher recognizes the difference between conjunctive, disjunctive and relational concepts. The conjunctive concept, in which the attributes add together to make the concept, is the easiest to learn. Most concepts are of this type. In contrast, the disjunctive concept is the most difficult to learn, as it is one which can be defined in a number of different ways. The rules of games contain disjunctive concepts. Since they are often 'culture bound' individuals from other cultures have the greatest difficulty in understanding the game, as for example, cricket in the case of the English.

More easy to learn are relational concepts such as distance and direction. They are important not only in geography but in everyday life. The difficulty that some drivers have in following directions is testimony to this fact. Culture is important in such learning: witness the difficulty that the British and Continental Europeans have with conversion between miles (imperial units) and kilometres (metric units).

Taken together all this information might seem to indicate that the best approach to the teaching of concepts will be simplification. It seems from work done by Bruner that individuals reduce the strain involved in dealing with several different attributes by reducing the number which they have to handle. Some pupils have difficulty in verbalizing concepts which they understand. This underlines the value of well designed classrooms tests as checks on performance. But there can be over-simplication to the point of confusion with other concepts. Certainly the 'noise' must be reduced: real life situations often produce too much noise because of their complexity, and pictures and diagrams can have the same effect. An outline diagram of a flower may be a better aid to pupil understanding of the parts of a flower than the flower itself. At the same time, a diagram which is complicated either by colouring or complexity may inhibit learning. Aids to learning need to be clear as well as simple; the same applies to blackboard work.

(This is not to deny the value of field studies in geography or biology particularly for urban children. The experience of such visits can be used as an advanced organizer for further study.)

Those pupils who are regarded by teachers as being less intelligent may be those who have difficulty in learning concepts as they are taught by that particular teacher. It may also mean that pupils are being asked to learn concepts which are too complex for them to grasp at their particular level of development (see section 5.5). It could also mean that too little time is allowed for their exploration and acquisition in the class. My own experience is that, in the name of the syllabus, too much is done in too short a period of time.

Another major problem for the teacher is the informal learning which has been done before the pupils come to his school or class. In particular the stereotypes which they have learned can hinder learning. A stereotype is a concept, already imbedded in the thinking of a pupil, which is generally impressionistic but not quite correct. The image of the role of the police that children who live in deprived areas in Britain and in the United States may have is an example. They may also have a stereotype of teachers which operates against learning, or of groups such as Jews and negroes. Stereotypes are also important factors in the perception that adolescents have about jobs and careers. At the same time, the fact that the concepts which pupils develop are limited by the experiences available to them illustrates the point that concepts cannot be learned without some relevant experience with the idea (phenomenon) which is to be conceptualized.

The main technique for the acquisition of concepts is the use of examples and non-examples. Their purpose is to help the pupil discriminate between appropriate and inappropriate characteristics of the concept. Teachers use both positive and negative examples, and the evidence supports the view that positive examples aid learning more than negative examples. When positive and negative examples are used, it seems that the best strategy is to precede the negative examples with positive instances of the concept. This reduces the demands which are placed on the learner. Learning is likely to take much longer when negative examples only are used. Exclusion strategies have to be used in certain activities as for example in medical diagnosis, and fault finding in cars and radios. Such strategies draw attention to the fact that learning a concept is a form of problem solving.

Too many examples of the same kind will lead to boredom. If, however, each new example provides new information then there is likely to be learning particularly if it is accompanied by feedback on the correctness or otherwise of the concept. Nevertheless, pupils do need to have practice with concepts. One investigation has suggested that distributed practice is better than concentrated practice. This reinforces the view that repeated study of concepts over a period of time helps concept formation. Teachers need to distinguish between memory and understanding. Often questions set in tests or class test recall (memory) rather than understanding (see Chapter 9). In classroom questioning it is likely that concepts will be reinforced if each answer is rewarded by the teacher with a remark similar to 'that's right' or 'that's wrong'.

Changes in subjects to be learned during the day may also have positive value, since they prevent teachers from doing too much. Change can also enhance learning, for if material which is similar to that associated with a concept just learned is given immediately after, that concept may be forgotten. The new material interferes with the previous material.

Brief reference was made in Chapter 1 to the interference which mathematics can cause in the understanding of physics. Price showed many years ago that students often get the formula right but the physical understanding wrong (reported by Heywood, 1974). Recent studies of this phenomenon have made use of recorded interviews of students thinking aloud (Newall and Simon). Clement (1981) gives some striking examples of the understanding of physics by freshman engineering students in the University of Massachusetts:

> Jim is asked about the concept of acceleration. He successfully
> differentiates an algebraic equation for the speed of an object to
> obtain the acceleration as a function of time. When asked, however,
> to draw a qualitative graph for the acceleration of a bicycle going
> through a valley between two hills, he confounds the concept of
> acceleration with concepts of speed and distance.

The basic concept is thus weak and undifferentiated. It is clear from the subsequent interview that Jim has both verbal and graphical difficulty with his explanation. All Jim has is a procedure for getting the right answer. He has so little understanding of the concept that he cannot apply it in a practical situation. Clement calls Jim a 'formula-centred student': His conceptual understanding is underdeveloped. Clement leaves the issue unresolved. It is a teaching problem even for the best teachers.

We may conclude that concepts are not 'just taught'. There are a range of strategies open to the teacher, some of which will be considered in the next chapter. An understanding of how they influence learning is essential for effective lesson planning and implementation.

5.8 Key concepts and the syllabus

The term *key concept* has been used in both America and England but in different ways. In both cases it seems to refer to complex issues which pervade the curriculum. Taba (1962) uses difference, multiple causation, interdependence and democracy as examples. In regard to the social science curriculum, she writes: 'These types of concepts are usually in the background and therefore often relegated to incidental teaching. In a sound curriculum development they should constitute (what some have called) *recurrent themes*, the threads which run throughout the entire curriculum in a cumulative and over-arching fashion.' The term 'key' is not introduced, although the significance of concepts as organizing elements in the design of the curriculum is readily apparent.

The Liverpool project reported in Blyth (1975) uses the key concepts in Exhibit 5.2. Their purpose is to help teachers choose, and organize, actual topics for work. The interpretation of a syllabus in terms of its concepts is an essential task for it helps teachers concentrate on those tasks necessary for understanding and the transfer of learning.

Key concepts mainly concerned with elements and processes in society

1. Communication — The significant movement of individuals, groups or resources or the significant transmission of information

2. Power — The purposive exercise of power over individuals, groups, or resources

3. Values and beliefs — The conscious or unconscious systems by which individuals and societies organize their response to natural, social and supernatural disorders

4. Conflict/consensus — The ways in which individuals and groups adjust their behaviour to natural and social circumstances

Methodological concepts mainly concerned with ways of analysing society

5. Similarity/difference — Classification of phenomena according to relevant criteria

6. Continuity/change — Distinction of phenomena along this essentially historical dimension

7. Causality — The notion that change in a state of affairs can be attributed to the phenomena preceding

---

Exhibit 5.2 *(reproduced by kind permission of the authors)*

References

For examples with explanatory criticisms of both Bruner and Piaget's work, see Biehler (1978); for technical explanations of their theories in relation to learning theory, see Hilgard and Bower (1975). On Piaget, for a philosophical criticism see Matthews (1980); for a psychological criticism see Brown and Desforges (1979); and for Piaget's views on mathematical education (and dissenting views) see Howson (1973). Most of Piaget's works have been published by Routledge and Kegan Paul, and see also Inhelder and Piaget (1958).

Some of Bruner's works are listed below. For a commentary on Lonergan and Whitehead see Heywood (1974).

R F Beihler (1978) *Psychology Applied to Teaching*. Boston, Mass: Houghton Mifflin, pp 112-67.

W A L Blyth *et al* (1975) *Place, Time and Society 8-13: An Introduction*. Bristol: Collins.

G Brown and C Desforges (1979) *Piaget's Theory: A Psychological Critique*. London: Routledge and Kegan Paul.

J Bruner (1960) *The Process of Education*. Cambridge, Mass: Harvard University Press.

J Bruner (1966) *Toward a Theory of Instruction*. Cambridge, Mass: Harvard University Press.

J Bruner (1972) *The Relevance of Education*. London: Allen and Unwin and Harmondsworth: Penguin.

J Clement (1981) Solving problems with formulas: some limitations, *Journal of Engineering Education*, 72, 158-62.

J Dewey (1930) *The Quest for Certainty*. London: Allen and Unwin.

R N Gagné (1976) *The Conditions of Learning* (3rd edition). New York: Holt, Rinehart and Winston.

J Heywood (1960) *Albert Einstein*. London: True Book Series.

J Heywood (1974) *Assessment in History*. Dublin: Public Examinations Evaluation Project, School of Education, University of Dublin.

E R Hilgard and G Bower (1975) *Theories of Learning* (4th edition). Englewood Cliffs, NJ: Prentice Hall.

A G Howson (ed) (1973) *Developments in Mathematical Education*. London: Cambridge University Press.

B Inhelder and J Piaget (1958) *The Growth of Logical Thinking from Childhood to Adolescence*. New York: Basic Books.

B Lonergan (1971) *Method in Theology*. London: Darton, Longman and Todd.

J MacMurray (1957) *The Self as Agent*. London: Faber and Faber.

G B Matthews (1980) *Philosophy and the Young Child*. Cambridge, Mass: Harvard University Press.

A Newall and H Simon (1972) *Human Problem Solving*. Englewood Cliffs, NJ: Prentice Hall.

M Shayer and P Adey (1980) *Towards a Science of Science Teaching*. London: Heinemann.

H Taba (1962) *Curriculum Development Theory and Practice*. New York: Harcourt Brace.

A N Whitehead (1932) *The Aims of Education*. London: Benn.

6 Learning from the Inside and from the Outside

6.1 Organizing questions

1. How do you account for the consistent results obtained in experimental studies showing that students who acquire generalizations through understanding are better able than those who do not understand such generalizations to use these generalizations in new situations where they are appropriate?

2. With reference to recent research and illustrations from your own work, discuss the role of discovery learning in the subject you teach.

3. 'I am not quite sure I understand what discovery is and I don't think it matters very much. But a few things can be said about how people can be helped to discover things for themselves' (Bruner). What are these things? To what extent do you think these views are supported by your research and your experience while teaching?

4. The film *Juggernaut* shows a bomb disposal squad dismantling a number of high explosives rigged on a passenger ship for its destruction. The learning process is clearly that of 'discovery' as the engineer seeks a way through the electro-mechanical timed firing circuits. Does this suggest that bomb disposal personnel should only be trained by discovery learning techniques? Your answer should be supported by references to recent research on instructional strategies.

6.2 Introduction

When learning theorists adopt a particular theory, they adopt a particular epistemological stance — that is, a theory regarding how things are known. Generally speaking, these views will be either in that tradition which can be traced back to Aristotle or that which can be traced back to Plato. The reason for the first organizing question of Chapter 5 should now be clear: I have argued in *Assessment in Higher Education* that the evidence supports an eclectic view of learning. We do, however, have to be clear about our position. As we shall see in the student responses which follow this section, a variety of instructional strategies seem to have worked in their classes.

Following Shulman, whose article (1970) on the evaluation of these different instructional strategies remains one of the best, the learning theorists whose work is contrasted are Bruner, Gagné and Ausubel.

Gagné's position is described by Shulman as neo-behaviourism, and is in the philosophical tradition of Aristotle. In this theory, the source of all knowledge is *experience*. The mind at birth is a *tabula rasa*, a blank slate on which are imprinted the effects of experience. The process of perceptual motor development can be interpreted in this way: we add to what has been learned before. As we shall see in the paragraphs which follow, Gagné's approach to the design of instruction is through learning hierarchies which move from the acquisition of simple to more complex skills, problem solving being the most complex of these. In this type of instruction, experience is highly organized, whether in classroom teaching or in programmed instruction.

Bruner's position is in marked contrast. It is a position within cognitive psychology. Shulman wrote:

> To understand the Bruner position on learning by discovery one must surely understand the pervasiveness of his Platonic idealism — a characteristic that sets Bruner apart from almost all other cognitive psychologists. We observed earlier that Bruner views the most fundamental and abstract ideas as inherently simple. Ultimate knowledge of these ideas consists of freeing oneself from the encumbering effects of their enactive and imaginal aspects and dealing with them in their purely symbolic, most efficiently transferable form. Most individuals have the 'basic stuff' of which these ideas are made, but must confront suitable problems or contrasts in order to clarify and restructure them. Hence, some variation of Socratic teaching suggests itself.

In this method, the purpose of teaching is to bring the learner to understand what he has always known. The mind contains all this information from birth; the learner has to discover for himself what is in his mind. Since knowledge, and the products of knowledge, are already in the mind, it is the process of the acquisition of these products, that is the process of knowing, which is all important. The only way that a learner can learn the process of knowing is by a process of discovery for himself. 'For Gagné the fundamental question is "What is to be learned?" For Bruner, it is "How do you get there and to similar places?" ' (Shulman).

As was shown in the earlier chapters the views we have about motivation are quite fundamental to the disposition we adopt in the classroom. The same is true of our views about the way people know. We will have an unconsciously formulated view about this which will influence our approach to lesson planning, implementation and discipline. Apart from discussion of moral issues it is this reason which makes the study of philosophy important in teacher training programmes, for we need to be able to explicate and support our view of the way people know. Shulman by implication illustrates this point and provides advanced organization for what is to follow:

A distinction originally made by Aristotle may be usefully invoked at this point. Aristotle distinguished between two different structures of knowledge: *ordo essendi*, the order of being, and *ordo cognoscenti*, the order of knowing. There is an important difference between the way things *are* and the manner in which they *become known*. Aristotle's implication is that we must distinguish between the structure of some knowledge in its fully developed form as grasped by the mature intellect and the structure of that same idea as it is presented for most effective and expeditious acquisition. Both Bruner and Gagné use the term *structure* in their writings; Bruner speaks of the centrality of the structure of the subject matter, while Gagné calls hierarchies 'learning structures'. In referring to the structure of the subject matter, Bruner collapses the distinction between the structure of being and the structure of knowing. The activities of the child and those of the mature scholar are to be quite parallel for Bruner, and will differ mainly in mode of representation used to cope with fundamental ideas or structures (see 5.3). In contrast Gagné clearly distinguishes between two kinds of structures. The order of knowing is reflected in the optimal sequence of a learning hierarchy. The order of being is a more abstract set of relationships that can only be comprehended when learning is complete. (*See below for illustration of a learning hierarchy.*)

Both Bruner and Gagné agree that the *processes* of acquiring and using knowledge are the most important forms of knowledge, in contrast to Ausubel, who believes that the understanding of the organized bodies of knowledge (ie subjects) are the main aims of education. He takes a *product* view of knowledge. These two positions have been greatly confused, as we shall see in the discussion on objectives in Chapter 8.

The contrasts between these three educationists may be illustrated from their own writings thus:

A body of knowledge, enshrined in a university faculty and embodied in a series of authoritative volumes, is the result of much prior intellectual activity. To instruct someone in these disciplines is not a matter of getting him to commit results to mind. Rather, it is to teach him to participate in the process that makes possible the establishment of knowledge. We teach a subject not to produce living libraries on that subject, but rather to think mathematically for himself, to consider matters as a historian does, to take part in the process of knowledge-getting. Knowing is a process not a product. (Bruner)

It may be argued, with much justification of course, that the school is also concerned with developing the student's ability to use acquired knowledge in solving particular problems, that is, with his ability to think systematically, independently and critically in various fields of inquiry. But this function of the school, although constituting a legitimate objective of education in its own right, is less central than its related transmission of knowledge function in terms of the amount

101

of time that can be reasonably allotted to it, in terms of the objectives of education in a democratic society, and in terms of what can be reasonably expected from most students. (Ausubel)

Knowing strategies, then, is not all that is required for thinking; it is not even a substantial part of what is needed. To be an effective problem-solver the individual must somehow have acquired masses of organized intellectual skills. (Gagné)

Bruner, as a result of his fundamental position, is led to the view that discovery approaches to learning will best meet his aim. Every-day life itself is a continuing process of discovery: for this reason discovery learning might be thought to be the best classroom strategy. While Gagné with Bruner emphasizes the importance of process, he like Ausubel believes that expository teaching will be more effective than discovery learning. So which is more effective? We turn first to the experience of the student respondents.

6.3 The experience of students with discovery learning and expository teaching

1. Gagné's hierarchical theory always works very well. Teach by using simple associations preceding higher level principles, etc. Found better transferability using this method when dealing with a particular topic, eg:

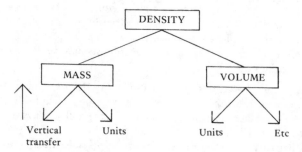

2. I use this method (discovery) quite successfully with first-year students but it has not been so successful with second years. I am led to believe that the reason for this is the fact that first-year pupils know no other method and seem willing to participate while the second-year pupils were used to other methods and resisted the demands made of them. Also, the instructional objectives for both classes are different; first-year requires more oral/aural practice, while second-year requires them to succumb to grammatical rules, essay-writing and translation. Accordingly, a different approach is required for second years, and this is one which is based on Gagné's and Ausubel's theories of carefully sequenced learning experiences.

An example from my class will elucidate these different theories.

The past tense (*passé composé*) has to be taught and this is the terminal behaviour. Prerequisite to learning this, recall of *avoir* and *être* are required. Then, verbs can be grouped into these two groups. The next step is agreement of the past participles, when and how they agree. This can be put into the sub-groups also. The final step is when to use the *passé composé*. This results in a hierarchy of learning tasks and the task at each level must be acquired before they can go on to the next level. Programmed foreign language courses have been designed by Carroll who even gives tests at the end of each stage for pupils and teacher to monitor progress.

An invaluable aspect of Ausubel's theory, the advanced organizer, has been very successfully implemented into the 'warm-up' session. Pupils can be introduced to the task and grapple with it before they meet it in all its nuances. For example, before teaching the past tense a few warm-up sessions would be spent on asking pupils 'What did you do yesterday?', etc. They are thus introduced directly to the new concepts which form the major part of subsequent instruction.

3. When conducting a poetry lesson with a first-year English class I adopted a Gagné type approach first of all to show the pupils how to analyse a poem. We began with the most basic questions about the meanings of words and progressed to types of words, rhyme, rhythm and eventually to style. At the end we were able to build up our answer from all the component parts to say what the poem was about and whether we thought it was good or not.

As we progressed with this type of exercise many of the basic facts could be left aside and I adopted another approach by which I would simply make a statement about the poem and expect the pupils to verify it if possible.

I found, however, that the lessons became very teacher-oriented and the pupils were afraid to commit themselves to an opinion unless first approved by me. I tried to change this by giving a test, an unseen poem which they had to 'solve' in a short space of time. The answers were, on the whole, positive and creative and produced a wider variety of 'solutions'. That would never have emerged in classwork. Furthermore when asked to recall any of the poems we had discussed, the unseen poem was most often remembered and the standard of work on poetry seemed to improve immensely after the 'Bruneresque' activity.

4. In science teaching one has to be prepared to use both methods of education. For example, take the Kinetic Theory of Gases. To teach this I found the most effective way was to use a structured approach as suggested by Gagné, working up from the fact that gases are made of atoms, to their motion, to what pressure is, etc, and the class were able to grasp the concept and finally we looked at Brownian motion.

At a later stage the class did Boyle's Law, but this time we did the experiment and the class were then guided by me asking questions and they worked back to the Kinetic Theory as explaining the Law. Trying to work back from the Brownian motion experiment did not work at all. In this case I had to change in the middle of the class and use Ausubel's advance organizer theory of using the experiment to set a scaffolding on to which I explained the theory.

Depending on what your aims are for a particular course or topic then the method of teaching that you use will vary. In some cases the process is important and in others the knowledge is important.

5. In language teaching it is important for pupils to be taught to use their own heads. Discovery methods do not necessarily imply a discovery in the external world and this is one of the 'things' that people can be taught — to say to themselves, 'Let me stop and think about that for a minute' and in this way to look to themselves, to discover within themselves. Children who wish to use a dictionary constantly might be better off either trying to recall the word or, if they have never learned it, to look at the context of the sentence and try and discover the meaning for themselves. In this way people are not only being helped to use their heads, but also to save time, perhaps to have more confidence in themselves and consequently more motivation to learn the language.

A second 'thing' that can help people toward discovery is to teach them to see the 'connectedness' between things. The pupils are taught to try to find connections between their past experiences, ie what they already know and new material. In language learning it is useful to give children phrases or new words and let them fit them into sentences they already know. This process means that they will assimilate new material more speedily and readily.

6. However, when I thought more carefully about his (Bruner's) statement that people can be encouraged to explore a situation I realized that some of the children in my class had already begun to do this in French and could be encouraged by questioning. One example is in the very arbitrary field of which nouns are masculine and which are feminine. At first this concept was totally alien to my class of ten- to 12-year-olds. Since English nouns were not all masculine or feminine they just could not conceptualize it. Not having come across this difficulty with other classes and having never experienced it myself, I did not know what to do, so we all discussed it in class and one pupil solved the problem by realizing that boat was *le bateau* whereas in English we refer to a boat as 'she'. Instantly everyone could make this concept his own because a parallel in his own experience had been found. Another boy noticed that *la voiture* followed the English 'she' for car. From then on everyone kept a watch for clues of the ways in which the French see their world and

experience. Perhaps this experience is more anecdotal than of educational value, but for me it opened a way to be aware of language not just as a way of saying things but as a way of experiencing things. Very often one imagines that this is above pupils' heads whereas in fact it may not necessarily be so.

7. As a teacher of French I can relate the audiovisual methods to the enactive level of strategy proposed by Bruner. The pupil seeing a flash card or picture is manipulating objects, as it were, seeing an object and learning a word at the same time. He will, we hope, come to the ikonic level where he can produce the word *livre* without seeing an actual book and later still, maybe, use the word without waiting for any mental picture of the object he wishes to talk about. Thus it seems to me ideal at the stage of Piaget's concrete operations to use such a method as Bruner's discovery learning. I can even do drills which facilitate this 'discovery':

> Je donne un livre *à Jean*,
> Je *lui* donne un livre,
> Je donne un cahier *à Marie*,
> Je *lui* donne un cahier,

and allow the students to 'induct' the rule.

8. After doing this I then approached the question of loyalty in a different way. I divided the class into small groups and we had an informal drama/role-playing session where the question of loyalty was again used. For instance, I had a mother interviewing her son on the whereabouts of his brother. The boy had promised his brother not to tell. In various situations the class faced questions of loyalty such as they were likely to have experienced. Afterwards we discussed what each group had found out. This could be called discovery learning in that while the pupils had previously experienced such situations, they now had the chance to verbalize them, to look at others' experiences, and to understand the different ways people had of responding. They had 'discovered' something. After this we went back to the text and discussed whether it revealed any new meanings. This sort of procedure I have found generally very useful in developing 'themes' or 'concepts' that I have chosen. However, when I have to deal with a complete play or novel, there are so many concepts depending on and influencing one another that I find straightforward discussion most effective for an understanding of the complexity and unity of the text. This need not be entirely expository, however, as comments and suggestions from the class are often a fruitful source of ideas.

9. In my own teaching subject, history, I have found that an expository teaching strategy is necessary for much of the time. History is not

a logical or rational subject in the sense that, say, mathematics is and it is necessary to derive information from the discoveries of others. The text that the class was using, however, was very abstract and most pupils ended up learning passages off by heart for exercise, rather than coming to a genuine understanding of history. To counteract this, I spent the second term doing a local studies project. This involved a type of discovery learning approach as I provided the children with various documents and maps, through which they built up a picture for themselves of the growth of Clontarf in the past 150 years. Bruner feels that pupils should learn the basic structures of a subject rather than the details which surround the structures. He feels that the study of history should involve the pupil in historical inquiry rather than in learning the results of such inquiry. In the case of my class of 12-year-olds, many developed a rudimentary notion of how an historian reconstructs the past: visits to the presbytery to see parish records, perusal of Griffith's Valuation Book to estimate population in the area and occupations of people, examining of different Ordance Survey Maps to explain the growth in population and occupations (location of beach nearby, building of Dublin-London Road in 1800, construction of railway line in 1841). Although much of this could be regarded as discovery work, it was very guided as pupils of 12 years of age needed help in organizing the data from documents and maps into meaningful structures. In particular, guided discussion helped many of them develop certain key concepts — continuity and change, cause and effect, power, values and beliefs. Without such guidance many would, I feel, have failed to accommodate the new experiences.

10. There are few people who would deny the value of an amount of discovery learning in a 'civilization' class for a group learning, for example, German. Bruner's approach would increase motivation, pupil activity and sustain interest, but it would also mean that a relatively small amount of information about, say, German towns, might take a relatively long time to acquire (children have to find books, look up ideas, etc). Hence the criticism that large-scale discovery learning is inefficient. On the other hand, it can be a welcome change and incentive, and lessons learned about independent or group work may, in the long term, be more important than what is learned factually. Thus, in an appraisal of the relative merits of the discovery method in the classroom, one must be very clear about one's exact objectives. Personally, I have great confidence in the benefits of discovery learning, provided that it is *one* aspect of classroom activity.

11. At all times, it is the process and not the product which is reinforced. Guided learning is cultivated. A prime example is where the methods of condensation and evaporation were taught and the

pupils then had to find out the separating technique of separating alcohol from water. This process of condensation was arrived at but the apparatus was crude, ie the use of a cold plate to condense. The pupils were then asked to think of an apparatus they could use to cool the 'steam' but *not* eventually condense it. However, by using their previous experience they did arrive at the concept. Furthermore motivation was extremely high during such a class and it was evident from the experimental work that transfer was maximized.

This method, therefore, of guided learning with an emphasis on process is maintained within the classroom. Unfortunately, not all subject areas can be studied in such a way, eg the circulation of the blood, and motivation was *not* as high when such an expository method was used in a subject that was deemed to have been interesting.

12. I have tried out Bruner's method of discovery learning by using worksheets in junior science classes. However, it is difficult to provide a 'pure' discovery situation in a classroom. The work cards provided minimal, but sufficient guidance to solving the problems at hand. I found that my pupils didn't take to the worksheets — possibly because they already had a particular learning set for science which was 'every other day laboratory work'.

13. At the time of teaching the concepts of atoms and bonding I brought models to the class and told the children to play with them. There were instructions on each box about colour, etc. The children messed about with the models (manipulative stage). Towards the end of the lesson I put H_2O, NH_3, CH_4 on the board and asked the boys to make models of these molecules using the equipment at hand. They completed this quite well (enactive stage). After a few more lessons during which they referred less and less to the models, I noticed more and more they were able to manipulate the symbols in the form of symbol chemical equations (symbolic stage).

14. Ausubel's ideas of meaningful guided learning I agree with and I tried this out in a class also. We were discussing the work carried out by Henry VII in England, placing particular emphasis on his economic policy. We learned the positive results of these deeds and then asked the girls to apply it to the situation Ireland finds herself in today. We spoke about promoting home industry, finishing off raw materials here so as to create employment, etc, just as Henry had done. But by learning in a meaningful manner they were able to apply these ideas to today. We also compared the voyages of discovery to the present and past space missions, and learned that similar problems are faced all the time by those making such new decisions. Again, this meaningful guided learning was applied to

methods of torture used by the Spanish Inquisition and used on the American hostages.

15. From application to the class it is clear that the nature of the subject matter has influence on the method of instruction used. Gagné's sequencing of skills is much more relevant to matter which has little form, little clear structure or clear conclusions. I found the discovery method very useful where what is to be learned has structure and is rational, eg interpreting ledger accounts back to source entries. It did instil enthusiasm, a sense of adventure and interest which helped motivation a great deal and is useful for this. However, it requires a lot of experience of dealing with discussion groups which I felt would have helped a lot had I had it. The students sometimes felt they were not going anywhere — my fault I know.

   Gagné's approach is very helpful for learning basic data which can be overlooked by kids left to discover.

6.4 Commentary

The four modes of teaching characterized in these responses may be categorized in terms of the way in which the teacher presents rules and solutions to the problems (Wittrock, 1963):

Type of guidance	Rule	Solution
Expository teaching	Given	Given
Guided discovery	Given	Not given (deductive)
Guided discovery	Not given	Given (inductive)
'Pure' discovery	Not given	Not given

The respondents also distinguish between rote and meaningful learning. In discovery learning trial and error procedures are meaningful; the memorization of mathematical tables is rote. Meaningful learning takes place when the pupils learn from the specific examples that there is a general rule. This is an inductive process. It contrasts with the pupil who in the deductive process has to solve problems of number series (see example at the beginning of Chapter 7).

The Joint Matriculation Board, Manchester, in its public examination at GCE Advanced Level in Engineering Science, makes a similar distinction for course work. It distinguishes between:

1. Controlled assignments: traditional laboratory practicals (two-hour activities)
2. Experimental investigations: discovery with advice available (6-12-hour activities)
3. Projects: discovery — carefully planned with advice available (50-hour activity).

Controlled assignments are laboratory practicals conducted with the aid of worksheets which have as their aims:

(a) the reinforcement and illumination of lesson material;
(b) the familiarization of students with the use of scientific equipment;
(c) the development of reliable habits of observation, confirmation and immediate record in journal style;
(d) the introduction of techniques in the development of skills of critical review, analysis, deduction and evaluation;
(e) the promotion of a good style of presentation.

The experimental investigation is an open-ended investigation in which the student is required to develop his own line of inquiry. It is intended to encourage students to devise experimental procedures, to select appropriate apparatus, occasionally to adapt pieces of equipment to new purposes, to perform experiments and to analyse results. It poses an engineering or scientific problem and involves the student in an analysis of the situation and an appropriate selection of the procedures and techniques for solution. The end point of the particular investigation may or may not be known but the means for its achievement are comparatively discretionary.

The project is a substantial exercise which involves the design, manufacture and evaluation of an artefact in 50 hours of laboratory time. In both experimental investigation activity and project activity there are substantial elements of discovery, although advice is available and careful planning is required. Although they have not been evaluated for learning retention, teacher and pupil attitudes have been obtained (Heywood, 1976). On the basis of such information the Board has seen no reason to change its procedures. Project developments in history have also been evaluated by the same investigator.

The student responses illustrate how ideas are put into practice, and some of the problems of applying learning theory to instructional practice. I doubt whether any of the students planned their approaches with the degree of sophistication undertaken by the theorists. It also seems possible to read into some of the responses that the technique eventually adopted arose more from the personal dispositions of the respondent than from objective evaluation of the results of research. There is also some misinterpretation among the respondents of Bruner's view that anything can be taught in a *meaningful way* to anyone. Bruner does not mean that everyone will be able to understand the totality of the subject. It does mean that everyone should be able to perceive the elemental principles on which the more detailed structures depend.

In its broadest interpretation, discovery seems to relate to the presentation of a problem to a pupil which the pupil then solves on his own. In a paper in *Nature* published about the same time as Bruner's *The Process of Education*, Heywood (1961) described project work by sixth formers (16-18 years) in England as meeting the principle of least learning. The students were given a substantive problem to solve with very little guidance. Many teachers have interpreted discovery learning in this way and it has justifiably met with much criticism, for unless the problem is clearly related to the entering characteristics of the pupils it is easy to deduce, as some of the respondents have done, that discovery learning is not suitable for the less able. But such conclusions are not justified by the evidence presented by other students or other investigations. Indeed, discovery learning has been shown to be very effective among adults who would have been classed as less able at school (Belbin and Belbin, 1970).

The need to clarify the meaning of discovery is to be found in Bruner's subsequent writings: his essays 'Some Elements of Discovery' and 'Toward a Disciplined Instruction' (Bruner, 1972) merit reading by every student teacher. He describes six aspects of learning which will help a person learn. These are:

1. the organization of learning so that the child recognizes that he can go beyond the information he already has (the attitude problem);
2. the organization of new materials so that the child is able to fit it into his own frames of reference (the compatibility problem);
3. the organization of the problem so that the child can perceive it to be within his own capacity to solve successfully;
4. the provision of training in the skills of information acquisition and problem solving, more especially in relation to the heuristics of the subject being studied;
5. aiding the child who can do things but who cannot convert what he does into a compact notion in his mind — Bruner calls this the self-loop problem;
6. helping the child learn skills for information handling.

Of these, (4) and (6) are of considerable importance, for they imply that training is valuable. Moreover, in the examples given in *The Relevance of Education* (1972), Bruner highlights the value of questioning. Children ought to be trained to test the limits of their concepts, to make hypotheses, and to be concise (ie to make the most of information). Such training, in my view, cannot always be by discovery, or if it is, it has to be evaluated. Bruner noted that while children find it relatively easy to make hypotheses, they find the testing of hypotheses much more difficult. The work on engineering science mentioned above confirms this view. I have argued that children have to be shown such skills, and that if discovery learning is to be successful the results of their exercises have to be evaluated, otherwise discovery learning can be an experience in which there is little learning.

The student respondents also said that discovery learning can be a lengthy process. But note should be taken of the use of questions in the language class as a form of guided discovery. There is also recognition that discovery learning can motivate some students.

The quantity of research on different learning strategies is comparatively small, which is perhaps surprising. Kersh (1962), in an often quoted experiment which sought to distinguish between rote learning, guided discovery and directed learning, produced inconclusive results which were nevertheless taken to heart by some of the respondents. The first was that explanation does not necessarily produce understanding. Hence the need to have our pupils evaluate our explanations. Secondly, he concluded that understanding and discovery methods do not necessarily prolong retention. I have suggested that a basic weakness of discovery learning is that pupils are not only often allowed to discover them without teacher evaluation, but that the correctly discovered is often not reinforced. Overall such evidence as there is suggests that some kind of guidance is likely to be more effective than no guidance at all. Minimizing the help given does motivate some students. But this may not be true of the less able pupil in regard to that particular subject. There is some evidence to support the view that generalizations/principles are understood better and retained longer when they have been learned inductively.

There is obviously much sympathy for the ideas of Gagné and Ausubel. They are (in particular Ausubel) related to the traditions used to teach many of the respondents! But it should be made clear that neither authority advocates a 'chalk and talk' approach. There is much more to learning than that, as the information in the previous chapters shows.

It is appropriate at this point to illustrate the approach to learning hierarchies. Gagné (1970) begins by defining the terminal behaviour. He gives the example of parallel parking a car. To arrive at this terminal behaviour the driver has to demonstrate motor skills (eg to move the vehicle in reverse at a low speed in the chosen direction), concepts (eg to identify the position for alignment with the other car) and component rules (eg to put the vehicle in the correct starting position). In Gagné's example there are four motor skills, four concepts and four component rules. Each motor skill and concept relate to one of the four component rules in a hierarchy.

A student respondent used this approach in the teaching of economics:

> The students are required to be able to analyse the demand and supply curves of a good in order to determine the equilibrium price and quantity. This is the terminal behaviour. Before this can be done certain concepts and skills must be acquired.
>
> *Concepts:* market, good, market demand, market supply, graph, demand curve, supply curve, intersection. (Note: the equilibrium price and quantity are found where demand and supply intersect, ie where demand = supply.)

In teaching this terminal behaviour to a fifth-year group one assumes that some subsets have already been acquired, eg drawing a line, the idea of 'equal to' etc.

Thus the behaviour to be acquired must be preceded by a number of subsets, which comprise the learning of concepts, eg 'demand', and the learning of skills, eg graphing points. During the process certain of these concepts will be defined and their definitions may be forgotten, eg price, quantity, market. But since the terminal behaviour is to find the equilibrium price and quantity, the students may be able to do this

TERMINAL BEHAVIOUR

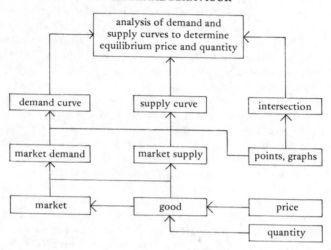

without necessarily remembering the definitions of, for instance, price and market. Thus if you have determined the terminal behaviour, *it is this which should be tested.*

This example differs from Gagné's in that the student has not distinguished between concepts and principles. This should be done in full. Moreover, it will be an advantage to show the pupils the hierarchy. One danger is that plans of this kind may require more than one lesson if the terminal goal is to be achieved in spite of prior knowledge.

In making a lesson plan it is useful to consider what the state of the blackboard will be at the end of the session. Exhibit 6.1 is taken from a lesson plan, also in economics, which had the aim of introducing the class to the use and function of simple index numbers. The overall purpose of a series of lessons was the understanding of the consumer price index.

Inflation	*Poster 1*	*Constructing a simple price index*	*Poster 2*	*Simple price index*		
general level of prices is rising	A simple price index		ZHIVAGO'S etc	Base year 1977=100		
		(1) base year — choose it		*1977*	*1978*	*1979*
		(2) find change in price etc		100	125	187
				1980	*1981*	
		Base year: 1977		212	262	
		% change in Price 1977/78: $\dfrac{2.50}{2} \times 100 = 125$				

Exhibit 6.1 *Blackboard at end of class*

As mentioned above, the student respondents felt that, by and large, weaker pupils benefit from a more expository approach to teaching. Some teachers experience difficulty in handling mixed ability groups; this problem is therefore briefly discussed in the next section.

6.5 Mixed ability teaching

(a) Organizing response

At present I am teaching a fifth-year geography class which has two other parts. One group is using mainly expository teaching because the class is slow and has a lot to catch up on in a short space of time. I am using a variety of techniques with a middle ability group which basically is guided discovery. The higher group is using more pure discovery methods and the application of discovered rules to different situations. All three methods were chosen to suit the needs and abilities of the pupils and accounting for the pressure of time and the length of the course.

(b) Commentary

Mixed ability teaching is a term which has come into use in Great Britain and Ireland as a result of the comprehensivization of school structures. A mixed ability group is a group of children representative of the whole ability range. Not only does the whole ability range have to be taken into account in teaching such classes, but also problems of personality have to be considered.

The report from the British Inspectorate (see last of the examination questions in the notes) suggested that a small number of enthusiasts were successfully undertaking mixed ability teaching. There is no doubt that its implementation requires extensive preparation, and its practice much patience.

Initially, the teacher requires a thorough knowledge of the entering characteristics of the pupils. The range of such information is wide. The pupil profile in Appendix 1 was developed to guide teachers in the acquisition of such information. Other profiles have also been developed, and those evaluated by Scottish headteachers are of special interest; these are more simple than the profile in the Appendix. Profiles demand systematic and more detailed record keeping than has been undertaken by teachers in the past.

The main difficulties in mixed ability teaching arise from the fact that many teachers find themselves directing their teaching at the large middle ability group. The bright group may cease to learn because of boredom. The less able may not receive adequate attention, and some children may perform badly because their difficulties have not been adequately diagnosed.

Bell and Kerry (1980) argue that the twofold distinction:

113

1. remedial (who might respond to coaching and return to the normal timetable),
2. less able,

is inadequate for the task. By implication, the profiles in the Appendix, which result from an evaluation of published research, support this view. Bell and Kerry suggest the following categories:

1. slow learner;
2. children with specific learning difficulties;
3. children with behavioural problems;
4. children who are socially and culturally disadvantaged;
5. children whose educational history is inadequate.

They then ask two questions of considerable value to the student teacher. These are:

1. The term 'slow' will not apply to all of a child's activities. Nor is slowness a bad thing. Could you write down three or four examples of slowness being a desirable characteristic?
2. *Think of a child* who is having problems generally with his/her school work. Write down as many observations as you can which seem to be related to his/her difficulties.

Later they ask the student teacher to check his or her observations against seven profiles under the headings: (1) academic performance/school work; (2) intellectual; (3) physical; (4) social; (5) emotional; (6) family background. These are very similar to the Murphy profile in the Appendix, but a weakness of their profile is that they do not take into account the effects of school environment and the teachers. Nevertheless, the teacher is likely to find that 'children who are lumped together as backward, when there is a smaller group, reveal wide differences in attainment. Catering for individual differences needs good preparation' (Bell and Kerry, 1980).

Specially trained remedial and guidance teachers are able to administer diagnostic tests for basic skills in reading, mathematics and spelling as well as social adjustment. Some specialists apparently keep test results from teachers. This seems a ridiculous practice, but it does mean that teachers must familiarize themselves with test procedures, analysis, limitations and potential at sufficient a level of understanding for them to understand the specialist's interpretation.

Bell and Kerry conclude their manual with the view that in the absence of hard evidence the teacher should:

1. prepare well for each class;
2. get down to the children's level of attainment;
3. make the pupils' work interesting;
4. find the things the children can do well so that success can breed success;
5. appraise his or her own behaviour;
6. assess progress, and try to ensure that some progress is made in each

lesson;

7. set simple targets for the pupils to achieve, remembering that their span of concentration is limited;

8. do not listen to staffroom gossip about a child without trying to make an objective judgement of his or her own.

At the other end of the spectrum are the very bright children. In the mixed ability group the teacher has to find a way of treating them with the same care and attention as the less able group. It came as a great surprise when I found that able children like structured teaching, particularly when they had experienced plenty of project work in the primary school.

One solution which has been adopted by teachers is the worksheet. This can be overused — Wragg (1976) headed an article 'Death by a thousand worksheets' — nevertheless, they do have a place in teaching.

Group practices have been widely used. There is much debate among teachers about whether pupils should be grouped by ability or mixed. Some of the student respondents had success with both types of grouping, while others found groups difficult to manage. One thought mixed ability teaching was only suited to more experienced teachers.

Individualized learning has also been practised with the aid of specially prepared kits. The SRA Reading Laboratory is an example.

I have always found (my first educational research was on mixed ability groups in a technical college) that the techniques, strategies and attitudes adopted for the less able were always appreciated by bright students. With this in mind it is appropriate to end with a lengthy extract from one of the student responses.

In my class of 32, I must first of all determine the range of ability (I'm teaching third form Latin; four are likely to get an A, four to get a vg, six a B, ten a C and the rest between D and E). This would be an approximate prognosis based on past exam performance and on one or two simple tests I would run in the class.

What are my objectives with this group? As many hons as possible — prestige, a high percentage of passes, general satisfaction. It is first of all important to look at the benefits that Latin can confer on each of these pupils, as a source of knowledge, a developer of skills, a way of thinking and a moulder of values. My general goal will be that each pupil will enjoy all of these benefits to a greater and lesser extent, independent of whether he/she is likely to get A or vg.

My behavioural objectives will be as follows: at the end of the school year each pupil will be able:

1. to translate x amount of Latin into English and vice versa (the amount will be determined in consultation with the teacher, and will vary from two pages of *Latin for Today* to 40 pages of *De Bello Gallico*).

2. to present a project (personally researched in conjunction with the teacher) on a topic of his own choice:

    (i) the life of Julius Caesar;

(ii) the relevance of Latin to a Dublin suburban schoolboy;

(iii) the influence of Latin on English;

(iv) Caesar's syntax;

(v) the Roman Empire and the SEC.

This will be worked on at home, in class and in the school library, done in a folder, with diagrams, pictures, cuttings, etc.

In this way each pupil will gain something personal for himself from the course, regardless of his ability. Its contents will be related to the next test as far as possible.

3. to present information as a member of a group for class discussion. The information will have direct bearing on the exam. In this way each person will be co-responsible for class performance in the exam.

4. to say what he got out of the class at the end of the year.

Learning strategies:

(i) work cards catered to individual learning needs;

(ii) regular formal input on basics;

(iii) individual assistance on project work;

(iv) assessment/monthly test to see if my objectives are being attained;

(v) collection of 'Latin-related materials, objects and information';

(vi) visits to museums/areas influenced by Romans.

If I can find an area of interest for each pupil, something that he is prepared to work on, then differential learning rates will not unduly retard a pupil or cause embarrassment to vg's.

6.6 A note on intelligence

When we speak of slow learners and/or the less able we refer, more often than not, to difficulties with reading, writing, communication and numbers. These are often related to the general factor of intelligence. Many British psychologists have looked at the abilities which people possess as forming a hierarchical tree, a model of which is shown in Figure 6.1.

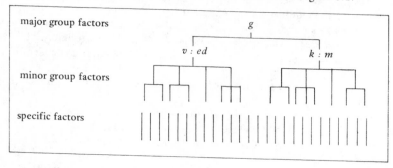

Figure 6.1

When the effects of g on a variety of performances have been taken into account there remain important groups of factors (major) which influence behaviour. Within these there are minor group and specific factors. The two major groups are $v : ed$ (verbal/numerical) and $k : m$ (spatial/mechanical). MacFarlane Smith (1964) has argued that (1) because the school curriculum concentrates on the verbal/numerical there is little development of spatial and mechanical abilities; (2) in consequence, in England and Ireland, the skills required for mathematics, science and technology are not highly developed; and (3) this accounts for the lack of interest in science and technology. There is some evidence to support the view that an improvement in spatial abilities among children in difficulties in the primary school may improve their overall performance.

Multiple aptitude tests, which test for a range of aptitudes, are widely used in schools for vocational guidance. The Differential Aptitude Test is widely used in schools in America where it was developed. It has been 'normed' for use in several other countries.

The American approach is very different although the techniques used are developments of factor analyses. The work of Guilford (1957) has been of particular interest to British teachers and investigators. Guilford classifies abilities under three headings:

(i) the basic psychological processes involved;
(ii) the kind of material content (eg letters, numbers and words when meaning as such is not considered);
(iii) the forms that information takes in the course of being processed, such as classes, systems, relations or transmissions.

(ii) and (iii) have been ignored by many of those interested in Guilford's work (especially teachers) because of the inclusion of divergent and convergent thinking in (i), which also incorporates cognition, memory and evaluation. Convergent and divergent thinking have been related to creativity and ability in science and technology. Hudson (1966) argued that school student scientists tended to be convergers and by implication that they would not be creative in design. This started off a lot of work on creativity in engineering (Gregory, 1974). From the point of view of teachers it is often argued that teaching methods tend to be convergent, that is, they support those pupils whose usual style of thinking is convergent. This means that those whose normal style of thinking is divergent are disadvantaged within the traditional curriculum.

6.7 General conclusion

The work of the Committees for the JMB Examination in Engineering Science (see 6.4), and the Research Unit of the Irish Public Examinations Evaluation Project, although aimed at the design of examinations, are based on the principle that for each educational (learning) objective to be attained there will be an appropriate instructional strategy from which will follow an equally appropriate method of assessment — as for example in the assessment of project work.

It is likely that in the future it will be possible, (given adequate information about the entering characteristics of the pupils) to delineate the learning strategy likely to be most effective in meeting a defined outcome. Shulman puts it thus:

> We need to think of instruction in terms of the selection of specific objectives and student characteristics. Our problem then ceases to be 'which method?' and becomes one of identifying the most effective sequences and combinations of methods for the achievement of a wide range of goals. (Shulman, 1970)

We shall return to this issue in Chapter 8.

References

M Ainscow and D A Tweddle (1979) *Preventing Classroom Failure: An Objectives Approach.* London: Wiley.

D P Ausubel (1968) *Educational Psychology.* New York: Holt, Rinehart and Winston.

E Belbin and R M Belbin (1970) *Retraining Adult Workers.* London: Heinemann.

P Bell and T Kerry (1980) *Teaching Slow Learners in Mixed Ability Classes: A Self-instructional Handbook of Strategies for Teachers and Student Teachers.* Nottingham University: School of Education Teacher Education Project.

J S Bruner (1960) *The Process of Education.* Cambridge, Mass: Harvard University Press.

J S Bruner (1972) *The Relevance of Education.* London: Allen and Unwin and Harmondsworth: Penguin.

H J Butcher (1968) *Human Intelligence.* London: Methuen.

B Davies and G Cave (1977) *Mixed Ability Teaching in the Secondary School.* London: Ward Lock.

R N Gagné (1976) *The Conditions of Learning* (3rd edition). New York: Holt, Rinehart and Winston.

S Gregory (1974) *Creativity in Engineering.* London: Butterworth.

J P Guilford (1957) A revised structure of the intellect, *Reports from the Psychological Laboratory of the University of California*, No 19.

G Haigh (1977) *Teaching Slow Learners.* London: Temple Smith.

J Heywood (1961) Research by sixth form boys, *Nature*, 191, 860.

J Heywood (1976) Discovery methods in engineering science at A level, *Bulletin of Mechanical Engineering Education*, 4 (2), 97.

J Heywood (1977) *Assessment in Higher Education.* London: Wiley.

L Hudson (1966) *Contrary Imaginations.* London: Methuen.

T Kerry and M Sands (1980) *Mixed Ability Teaching in the Early Years of the Secondary School: A Teaching Practice Workbook.* Nottingham University: School of Education Teacher Education Project.

B Y Kersh (1962) The motivating effect of learning by directed discovery, *Journal of Educational Psychology*, 53, 65.

I MacFarlane Smith (1964) *Spatial Ability.* London: University of London Press.

P Newbold (1978) *The Banbury Report.* Windsor: National Foundation for Educational Research.

L S Shulman (1970) Psychology and mathematics education, *in* E G Begle (ed) *Mathematics Education.* Chicago, Ill: University of Chicago Press/National Society for the Study of Education.

P Westwood (1975) *The Remedial Teacher's Handbook.* Edinburgh: Oliver and Boyd.

M C Wittrock (1963) Verbal stimuli in concept formation: learning by discovery, *Journal of Educational Psychology*, 54, 183-90.

E C Wragg (ed) (1976) *Teaching Mixed Ability Groups.* Newton Abbott: David and Charles.

Examination questions related to mixed ability teaching

1. Outline British and American approaches to the study of intelligence. What insights into the behaviour of children do you think they give and what implications do they have for you in the planning of your curriculum?

2. What implications does the theory of convergent and divergent thinking have for the organization of your teaching? Illustrate your answer by examples from your own experience.

3. 'Mixed ability and mixed temperament' is a better phrase than 'mixed ability' to describe the problem facing many teachers. Why should this be? Support your answer by reference both to reported research and your own experience.

4. Do older buildings and classrooms necessarily mean 'traditional methods'? Discuss ways in which old facilities and accommodation may enable teachers to overcome the limitations placed upon their classroom work with groups of mixed ability children.

5. Discuss the relevance of perceptual learning theory in the education and training of the slow learner.

6. Read the following passage carefully and answer the questions relating to it which follow the passage:
    (1) Mixed ability teaching rarely produces satisfactory results at secondary school level, the English School Inspectorate says in a background document prepared for the Government's conference on comprehensive education.
    (2) Teaching groups of children of a wide range of ability made demands on teachers that were extraordinarily difficult to meet, especially at secondary level, the Inspectorate says.
    (3) 'The outcome, with few exceptions, where highly gifted enthusiasts have given much time and effort to careful planning and preparation and have built in continuing and effective assessment procedures, is one of two kinds of unsatisfactory practice.'
    (4) In one, where traditional teaching methods appropriate to groups of mixed ability were preserved, demand was pitched at some estimate of 'the middle', with almost certain failure to satisfy either extreme of the ability range, the Inspectorate says.
    (5) That difficulty might be partly concealed in schools that were comprehensive in name only, containing few if any of the most gifted pupils. The effects of the stress at both ends might become more apparent, however, when the full range of ability was present.
    (6) In the other approach, 'teaching' almost vanished, yielding to individualized learning techniques, generally based on assignment cards and worksheets that were not always of adequate quality.
    (7) Such devices, when well prepared, carefully chosen and wisely used, could make a significant contribution to the difficult task of matching demand with capacity, but it was important to realize the limitations of such methods. Even the best individual programmes provided only one kind of learning experience, the Inspectorate says.
    (8) Some argued that total mixed ability teaching throughout a school was the only way to implement comprehensive philosophy and thus ensure equality

of opportunity. However, it could rarely guarantee the latter, since its operation normally involved the deployment of teachers, who were demonstrably unequal in quality, on the carefully 'equalized' teaching groups.

(9) The Inspectorate's strong reservations about mixed ability teaching certainly does not mean that it favours the opposite extreme, that of streaming or the strict division of children according to their supposed general ability into separate classes for all subjects.

(10) The argument against streaming, that pupils tend to fulfil what is expected of them, had now won general acceptance, the Inspectorate says. It was also widely recognized that streaming could take no account of the strengths and weaknesses of an individual in different subjects.

(11) Comparatively few schools had gone over to total mixed ability teaching, even in the first three years. Most schools had adopted compromises between the two extremes, such as 'setting' by ability in particular subjects like French and mathematics, or broad banding, which still remained vulnerable to the expectation-fulfilment charge. There is no ideal solution, the Inspectorate says.

(12) Turning to another recent trend in schools, the great increase in attention given to the social and personal development of a child, the Inspectorate suggests that there might now have been too big a swing in the direction of pastoral care at the cost of academic standards. Teachers' time was the main constraint, it says.

(13) The Inspectorate clearly does not want to suggest that pastoral care is unimportant, simply that it should be kept in balance with academic considerations within the limits set by a school's resources. Indeed, one of the five papers in the Inspectorate's report is devoted entirely to pastoral care.

(14) Few would disagree with the Inspectorate's statement that the prime purpose of school is to be an agent for learning.

(15) But it was important to be aware of the extent to which social and personal factors bear on a child's learning performance, and vice versa, and of the need actively to provide opportunities for all pupils, whatever their ability, to grow to personal and social responsibility in a supportive yet not overbearing atmosphere.

The other four papers in the 62-page report deal with the curriculum; the internal organization of school, including teaching methods; pupils with special needs; and the wide variety of patterns of comprehensive schools. The Inspectorate's conclusion on the last subject is that 'no single pattern has the monopoly of advantage'. (From *The Times*)

(a) What do you understand the Inspectorate to mean by mixed ability teaching? (para 1)

(b) What do you understand the Inspectorate to mean by traditional teaching methods (para 4)

(c) (i) What do you understand by individualized learning? (para 6)
(ii) What do you understand by assignment cards and worksheets? (para 6)
(iii) How would you distinguish between the quality of good and poor assignment cards and worksheets?

(d) 'Even the best individual programmes provided only one kind of learning experience' (para 7). What other kinds of learning experience would you expect to be provided for mixed ability groups?

(e) Differentiate between (a) streaming, (b) setting, and (c) banding.

(f) What do you understand by the term 'general ability'? (para 9)

(g) In what ways has more attention been paid to 'the social and personal development of the child'? (para 12)

(h) What do you understand by the term 'academic standards'? (para 12)

(i) What do you understand by the phrase 'to grow to personal and social responsibility in a supportive yet not overbearing atmosphere'? (para 15)

(j) How do social and personal factors bear on a child's learning performance and vice versa? (para 15)

7 Problem Solving

7.1 Organizing questions

'All teaching predisposes learners to develop rather restricted skills in analytical thinking' (Heywood, 1978). With reference to problem-solving behaviour discuss this view in relation to your own teaching.

Describe an experiment which illustrates the influence of a 'set' in solving problems. How would you distinguish between good and poor problem solvers and what steps would you take to encourage fresh approaches to problem solving?

There is substantial agreement among investigators about the major steps taken by individuals when solving problems. What implications has this theory for training pupils in the project method and the subsequent assessment of their work?

What specific problem-solving skills are available to be learned in your subject? How do these skills contribute to the learning of general problem-solving processes? Illustrate with concrete examples.

'Both industrialists and teachers misunderstand the role of education in preparation for work and life.' Discuss this statement in the light of recent research and development on the teaching and learning of problem-solving skills.

7.2 Steps in problem solving

(a) Organizing response

The first-year history programme exposes the children to so many new concepts that quite a lot of expository teaching has to be engaged in. In teaching a concept like 'Renaissance' or 'Revolution' my teaching is mainly expository. At other times I set up problem situations, eg 'When the Third Estate arrived at the Estates General meeting place they found the doors locked. They did not go home but went to a tennis court close by and resolved not to disband until a constitution was written and they got their demands.' In a problem situation like this I ask the children to identify the problem, to analyse it, to make hypotheses and to find possible solutions.

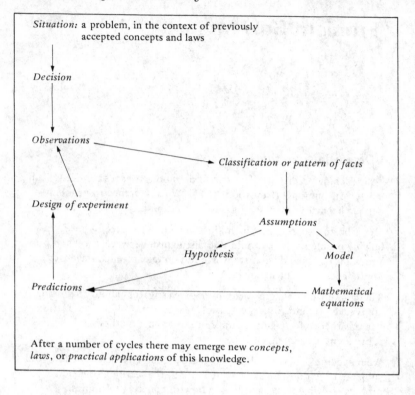

Situation: a problem, in the context of previously accepted concepts and laws

Decision

Observations

Classification or pattern of facts

Design of experiment

Assumptions

Hypothesis

Model

Predictions

Mathematical equations

After a number of cycles there may emerge new *concepts, laws,* or *practical applications* of this knowledge.

Exhibit 7.1 *Solving a problem in science* (from Heywood and Montagu-Pollock, 1977)

(1) Ability to recognize the existence of a problem

(2) Ability to define the problem

(3) Ability to select information pertinent to the problem

(4) Ability to recognize assumptions bearing on the problem

(5) Ability to make relevant hypotheses

(6) Ability to draw conclusions validly from assumptions, hypotheses and pertinent information

(7) Ability to judge the validity of the processes leading to the conclusion

(8) Ability to evaluate a conclusion in terms of its assessment.

Exhibit 7.2 *Steps involved in critical thinking* (from Saupé, 1961)

(b) Commentary

There is much agreement among investigators about the steps involved in solving a problem. As the respondent indicates, it is necessary to identify the problem, analyse it, make hypotheses and test their solution. This process involves feedback, and is similar to the cybernetic model of decision making. It is in this sense that learning and decision making can be said to be the same thing (McDonald, 1969).

Exhibit 7.1 shows a model of how a scientist might go about solving a problem (Heywood and Montagu-Pollock, 1977). You will see that each activity is itself a skill. Saupé (1961) has argued that all the evidence leads to the view that skills in problem solving (critical thinking is sometimes used instead of problem solving) are improved if the learner has a model, or knowledge of the steps in the process. His list is given in Exhibit 7.2.

Highlighting the skills should assist their development. One way of achieving this is to devise assessment procedures which will highlight the acquisition of skill within a subject rather than the recall of knowledge. Projects are an invaluable aid in this respect: while they draw out understanding as Bruner would advocate, they emphasize equally the skills which are the products of learning. It is in this sense that there is no conflict between the process and product approaches to learning. Schemes of assessment for project work which highlight both process and product have been designed and evaluated for engineering science (17- to 18-year-olds), and history (15-year-olds), and are explained in detail in Heywood (1978).

But this approach need not be confined to projects. A weakness in using essay-writing (whether for short stories, narrative, or reporting) is that teachers too often assume that pupils know how to write essays. In consequence they do not provide adequate correction. Such correction can be assisted by a detailed marking scheme which the pupils are shown. One cannot over-emphasize the value of relating the assessment procedure to the teaching strategy and of showing the pupils quite clearly what is wanted for each particular grade. Clearly the procedures for assessing a novel will differ considerably from those for assessing a scientific project except in its creative aspect. There is always a danger that these procedures will inhibit personal development, but once the teacher is aware that this may be the case countervailing action can be taken, as is shown in the next section.

7.3 Creativity and teaching method

(a) Organizing responses

1. Convergent thinking is encouraged by the examination system. In the language domain marks are awarded for 'aspects of language' (eg style, vocabulary, grammar). This serves as an impediment to creative thinking, and even worse, to language as a means of communication.

De Cecco and Crawford suggest certain steps for effective problem solving in the classroom. The teacher should analyse the problem, help with the recall of the various concepts and principles involved, structure them and evaluate them.

According to Gagné, 'creativity' is an intuitive leap in problem solving. Creativity, say de Cecco and Crawford, is rarer than intelligence and involves such factors as originality, fluency and flexibility. Creativity must be encouraged. To a certain extent the pupil has the chance to be creative in the essay choice of Intermediate/Leaving Certificate Papers (eg (1) (*Critical*): Discuss road accidents in Ireland; (2) (*Creative*): Write a story 'A Day on a Farm').

Critical thinking is problematic in that many pupils have missed out on the earlier stages of concepts and principles. I have found that there is little point in a question such as 'Let us consider this text in terms of style' when the concept of style may be lacking in the pupil's conceptual repertoire. So the teacher begins again. Up the Gagné pyramid . . . but he/she must try to prevent set learning (if it becomes too inhibiting). This I think can often be done by respecting the pupil's own powers (often they are far more creative than the teacher's) and by working as a team and respecting each other's point of view set induction will surely be reduced.

2. In the classroom we tend to have stereotyped ways of problem solving. By this I mean that we don't allow for variety but for direct and straightforward answers. The example that springs to mind is in the type of homework I gave to pupils in the first term. They were all straightforward questions on stating principles, same parts, etc. When I gave a question on the parts of the skeleton one child decided to give a lively imaginative type of essay. Only then did it occur to me that I was restricting the children by the nature of the questions. I wasn't allowing for fun, for imagination or for enjoyment. After this my lessons have varied from questions like 'what happened to the meal I ate' to 'the latest experiment we did in class'. The phrasing of the homework or of questions did not allow for creativity and imagination which are both forms of problem-solving behaviour. They did not allow for fluency of thought or creative thinking but rote-type learning which was forgotten easily.

The reader by now will be aware that the focus in this approach to classroom management leads necessarily to the view that lessons have to be carefully planned. If such planning is to be successful then the aims and objectives have to be spelled out with clarity.

These illustrations are a reminder of the convergent/divergent issue (see Chapter 6) and the fact that our teaching strategies can limit children's thinking in the classroom. When this happens we impose restrictions on their ability to develop learning skills. It also illustrates how easy it is to create such restrictions, as for example in questioning (see Chapter 5). Questioning is a skill which can be learned. The teacher needs to have a profound awareness of its effects. We all need to be reminded (first respondent) to respect the pupil's own powers of creativity.

7.4 Set induction in problem solving

(a) Organizing responses

In comprehension problems in English, from my experience children are largely incapable of deducing from a fairly long passage the essential points. In second language teaching the subjects find a common word in the question and in the comprehension passage and copy large sections of irrelevant material rather than analysing the situation. Students are also disinclined to use fresh approaches in the use of words in certain 'sets' rather than applying them to new situations.

We give pupils learning sets — which due to familiarity, stereotyping and fixed modes of thought hamper ability to attack a problem. Davis suggests 'torpedoing' as a solution. If one problem is given which looks similar to the others given but which in fact demands a different approach, a pupil is forced to seek a new method of solving it. If, for example, in a list of authors or poets, she includes a misplaced person's work or piece of writing that is not typical, a student is in the situation of analysing it.

On working with number series in my own class I tried using discovery techniques. The class were given the number series and asked to complete them without any help which most managed. When they were given a second number series there were more problems. The vast majority attempted to apply the same type of rule which had solved the first problems to them only to find that it did not work. They had as such become 'set' in their thinking.

First series
$n_2 = n_1 + n_2$ 2 4 6 8 10 12

Second series (more difficult)
$n_3 = 3n_1$ 2 4 6 12 18 36

(b) Commentary

My first introduction to the idea of set in problem solving was in a paper by Furneaux (1962). In a factor analysis of engineering examinations in a university he showed that each examination (whether it was mathematics, aerodynamics or electricity and magnetism) tested the same thing. I came to the conclusion that, because the solution of engineering science problems for a single answer depended on the application of a limited range of mathematical techniques, the examination papers were testing a specific type of analysis. This led me to try to design examination papers which tested a wide range of skills, first in engineering and subsequently in history and mathematics. While these sub-tests apparently tested different skills, I am not sure that the overall skill tested was a generalized kind of analysis — except in project work. We tend to teach in an analytic and convergent mode. It is the divergent mode in which the development of skills of synthesis is likely to occur.

The experiment to which the examinees referred was by Luchins and is described in many textbooks. He asked pupils in his research group to obtain specified amounts of water from three jars filled to different levels (capacity). He showed them first how to do two problems which involved all three jars. In a further nine problems, the subjects mainly used the three-jar solution, to solve the problem even when two-jar solutions were possible. The 'set' interfered with their problem solving. Subsequently Luchins divided another group into two sub-groups. The first sub-group worked through the problem in the usual way, using the three-jar solution. The second sub-group were told to think more carefully about how to solve the problems. Given that instruction, the majority of students in the second sub-group moved to the more simple solution of using two jars. Some of the respondents refer to the 'torpedo effect' which is intended to change a person's 'thinking approach'. Wittrock has suggested that 'sets' can also assist learning. He cites research on advanced organizers to this effect. Note also the apparent ease with which 'sets' can be established (third respondent). Examination questions of the kind I developed were designed to induce particular 'sets'. Familiarity increases the likelihood of a 'set' becoming a controlling influence. Teachers should try to design problems for which there are several different methods of solution so that students become aware that most complex problems and indeed many simple ones can be solved in a number of ways, some of which are likely to be more simple than others. Sets may have a positive or negative effect on learning.

7.5 Success and failure in problem solving

Individuals react to success and failure in solving problems in a variety of ways. In general, success is likely to breed success (see Chapter 2). Failure, on the other hand, can lead to maladaptive behaviour. Some people, for example, will continue to repeat a task in the same way and fail to reach a solution. Some persist with a task even though they know it will produce a wrong answer. Sometimes this is because the problem solver is afraid (see first respondent, section 7.6). Sometimes it is because he has used the method before, and feels it ought to work now. Sometimes there is a substitution. The problem solver is hurt by frustration. To reduce the pain he substitutes another goal in order to reduce its intensity. This occurs when a person fails university entrance examinations which lead to a specified career strongly embedded in his mind. Failure means that he has to specify another career.

Aggression is another well known reaction to failure in solving a problem, as are dependency reactions, although to seek the help of another is not maladaptive. From the teaching point of view failure to solve classroom problems can lead to frustration, aggression, and in consequence more failure. The teacher therefore has to begin by setting problems which the child can solve. In this sense the idea that each class (even though it is selective) is mixed ability is important, since it is a reminder to the teacher to select questions appropriate to the characteristics of the child being questioned.

7.6 Problem solving in groups

(a) Organizing responses

I will now discuss with reference to a first-year class I have been teaching of 30 pupils, all girls, who had been accustomed in primary school to a form of learning whereby the teacher sat or stood at the top of the class and the children sat in rows of desks, two in each desk.

These young people were frightened by new experiences, even the simple one of suggesting that our tables and chairs might form a U-shape rather than regular rows.

They coped by withdrawing — putting their heads down, or interestingly going to the other end of the continuum and becoming openly hostile and aggressive.

They were afraid to think. The research of Osborne on group problem solving I found particularly helpful. I discovered after consistently encouraging the class to work in groups of three or four that:

☐ their level of motivation increased markedly
☐ they had the opportunity to communicate together as a group, with each other and then with the whole class
☐ frustration was reduced as the tasks were shared among the group members
☐ leadership emerged and other roles were assumed by the girls to complete the tasks.

As a result I feel that these young people now can attack a problem, task or whatever goal needs to be attained and attempt several different behaviours to arrive at their goal. They no longer rely on one set.

When a teacher decides that a class is to solve a problem and if the problem is highly complex he might decide to divide the class into groups. Preferably, when the class is divided into groups, the complex problem is simplified by members in the group, group work encourages communication and this helps solve problems. Leadership is also important in group work so one might do the questioning and get out the answers, whereas if working individually, a pupil might not think of the same answer.

In my classes I found group work most rewarding amongst the class doing English poetry. Trying to solve the problem of exactly what the poet is trying to get across, the class divided into groups, each being given a leader. A problem was written on the board and the class asked to find the solution to the problem, 'What is the poet really trying to get across?' I found a wide range of ideas, 60 per cent abstract and negative, and 30 per cent positive and abstract.

Experiment — of group work in which I asked students to identify examples of fascism from a given set of imagined situations. The lesson branched into considerations of other political terms such as dictatorship and generated some heated argument in which underlying percepts emerged. It was an extremely useful lesson for the reasons claimed by the experiments of the brainstorm technique:

☐ range of suggestions,
☐ encouraging thinking,
☐ differentiating in the sense that is an essential part of conceptualizing.

(b) Commentary

These teachers have found group problem solving to be effective. Groups can be more effective than individuals at solving a problem. They are widely used in management training. Apart from anything else, group work should assist the pupils to work in a team. Groups have the effect of minimizing individual frustration but in so doing they may help a person avoid the task which is to be done. Most of the respondents who described their work with groups found that the assignment of pupils to groups was not an easy matter. As with all other techniques of instruction the teacher needs to be clear about the objectives for group work. It is to accomplish 'affective' objectives as is often the case in management? For example, will the purpose be to learn to work in a team? Or are the objectives to be cognitive? For example, will the purpose be to learn how to generate alternative solutions to the problem?

There are many ways of organizing groups and there are several techniques available for use in group problem solving. One of these is *brainstorming*. When this technique is used the participants generate as many ideas as possible in a limited period. These are then subjected to evaluation in order to find a suitable idea for subsequent development.

Sometimes a class can be divided into groups. Each group is asked to solve the same problem. At the end of the allotted period each group presents its solutions (views). This can be a very rewarding procedure, since if the problem is carefully chosen it is likely that the groups will produce different insights into the problem.

7.7 Problem levels

The difficulty with the Gagné model of problem solving is that it can lead to the view that understanding a concept is not a problem. Similarly, some situations which are apparently S-R may present quite serious problems to some individuals. We cannot always assume that all persons in a class will perceive an issue to be a problem. They may simply regard the matter as a straightforward acquisition of knowledge. As has been mentioned, the understanding of an examination question can be a major problem. The way in which we perceive problems seems to relate to the perceived level of difficulty. It will also depend on our entering characteristics. These will include not only our formal learning but our informal learning, interests, abilities and personalities. All this serves to reinforce the view that in problem-solving activities the teacher must cater for the needs of the individual student.

7.8 Overview

'Unfortunately', writes a teacher of engineering in the United States, 'many instructors cannot see it [problem solving] as an educational problem, feeling that students unable to work problems just do not understand the subject material' (Red, 1981). However, like many other trainers in engineering and management, Red took the opposite view, that students *could* be trained in problem solving. Like others he had applied the heuristic developed by Polya (1957) for problem solving in mathematics. Polya's plan is in four stages:

1. Understanding the problem
2. Devising a plan
3. Carrying out the plan
4. Looking back.

His book begins with a list of basic injunctions. One of the injunctions highlights the value of analogy thus:

> If you cannot solve the problem try to find some related problem that is related to the auxiliary problem, which we consider not for its own sake, but because we hope that its consideration may help us to solve another problem, our original problem.

This has an affinity with the methods of assessment used in the engineering science projects to which reference has been made. It is similar to the process of design, my view of which is shown in Exhibit 7.3. It is also similar to the scientific problem process shown in Exhibit 7.1.

If we look at the skills involved in design we see that it is possible to provide specific training in each area. This project planning uses among other skills:

☐ the ability to form a hypothesis
☐ the ability to form a specification from a hypothesis

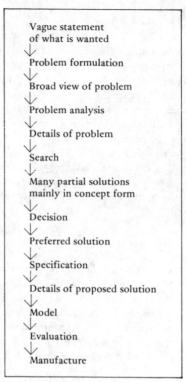

Exhibit 7.3 *A model of the design and manufacturing process*
(Krick, 1966)

☐ the ability to describe alternative solutions to solve the hypothesis
☐ the ability to evaluate those alternative solutions and so on.

These skills embrace, of course, the skills of critical thinking listed in Exhibit 7.2, and they can be applied to the methodology of most subjects. An interesting development of this idea is life skills teaching within career education (Hopson and Scally, 1981). The evaluation of history projects referred to in *Examining in Second Level Education* (Heywood, 1978) shows that history teachers had little difficulty in modifying the scheme of assessment in engineering science to meet the needs of history.

Red (1981) suggests that Polya's approach does not work satisfactorily unless the students are given detailed instructions for each step of the strategy. This he did in his laboratory work. Thus at the plan stage, which is the final step in his heuristic, the students were instructed as follows:

Write down the equations from which the unknowns can be found using the given information. These equations are the connection between the given data and the unknowns:

Then:
(1) Carry out the plan ie apply the equations
(2) Check each step
(3) Underline or block in each answer so that it is easily identified
(4) Make sure that each answer meets with common sense ie is it realistic? Then make sure each answer satisfies the assumptions and conditions stated for the problem.

The assessment procedures for projects simply turn these statements into questions. Can the candidate do this or that? For example:

Analysis and synthesis. (Analysis is a preliminary step to arranging the material collected in a coherent pattern. It involves the selection of the most important and relevant points from the information assembled. Synthesis is the expression of the pattern that emerges from the analysis of the subject matter.)

This candidate (referring to the assessment of a history project):

☐ made no attempt at analysis
☐ fails to distinguish relevant from irrelevant material and issues and important from unimportant material and issues
☐ distinguishes some important issues arising from his topic
☐ has isolated the important issues, factors or questions arising from his topic.

This candidate:

☐ shows little attempt to organize the material collected
☐ has organized his material into a coherent pattern
☐ has organized his material to answer questions or to describe issues, or to explain factors involved in the material.

Such questions force the candidate to think about the skill which is to be developed. One cannot hope to validate all the effects of a project in an esaily administerable instrument. However, one can hope to choose half a dozen or so key skills which in their performance will use many other lower order skills.

My own work suggests that less able pupils have great difficulty in formulating a problem. They cannot get beyond a rather vague title, and also have difficulty in recognizing the assumptions which they make. All students, whatever their ability, have difficulty in evaluating their own work, and training has to be given in these areas. The teachers of engineering and history with whom I have worked have found that the assessment procedure is enhanced if the students prepare a plan which forecasts what they are going to do in some detail. In the GCE examination (and our experimental examinations) these plans are submitted to an assessor. A pupil cannot proceed with a project without the agreement of the assessor who tries to ensure that the project is viable within the time allowed. Viability is the likelihood that the topic chosen and the plan submitted will, if the project is done effectively, gain the student marks in all the skill areas of the assessment. Holt (1977) calls this a morphological technique.

But this is by no means the whole story, for the context in which the problems are set can vary immensely. In the preceding discussion, reference has also been made to problem solving in projects which take 50 hours. For the most part life is made up of a wide range of relatively small problems in terms of the time required for their solution, but they may create as much strain as the problem which has to be solved in the long term, and pre-occupies us over a long period.

If problem solving is learning, so is decision making, which is in effect the outcome to the solution of a problem. Indeed, decision making may be a more appropriate expression of our daily activity.

Most of my work has been done with individual projects. Teachers have found the 'brainstorming' technique referred to in section 7.6 a valuable aid to pupils who are having difficulty in generating ideas. Some sophisticated approaches have been developed to group problem solving. In management, for instance, a technique has been developed for stimulating individuals when they are at their most creative. It is called 'synectics' (Holt, 1977). It seems to me to employ the Polya type heuristic in a group. One week's training is usually given to industrialists who want to use this technique. It is difficult to employ, but it might be modifiable for the classroom.

Briefly, in this technique, the pupil who cannot decide what to do for a project presents a vague idea to a group about what he wants to do. The group begins by discussion and analysis. They next eliminate immediate and obvious solutions. The purpose is to test preconceived ideas (see Chapter 4). A statement of the problem as understood is then obtained.

At fifth stage, the chairman tries to stimulate divergent thinking. He or she asks for a solution in one of these analogies:

1. *personal analogy*, where the problem solver identifies himself with the object or situation and imagines how he would react;
2. *direct analogy*, where biological, mechanical or other solutions to similar problems are examined;
3. *symbolic analogy*, in which the crucial or unclear parts of the problem are symbolized in words, pictures or other images.

(There may be an analogy here with Bruner's modes of learning.)

Under the questioning of the chairman, the group develops analogies in relation to the problem as they understand it until a problem is found. Whitfield (1975) describes this technique in detail.

Experience suggests that groups of people often solve problems in this way. Pupils might be trained in such methods and in the chairmanship role. Like other problem-solving techniques developments will inevitably take place in the cognitive as well as the affective domains.

Returning to the classroom, a variety of simulations have been devised for this use and much has been written about them. Role-playing exercises are commonly used in language teaching; case studies and business games are commonly used in schools, and some decision-making games have been specifically designed for school use.

Most problems require both analytic and associative thinking skills. Whitfield argues that the design process (or creative process) which was outlined above can be viewed as a sequence of activities which require both convergent and divergent thinking. He relates each stage to desirable personal characteristics, supporting techniques (of which many more are discussed than are mentioned here) and methods for personal development.

For example, at the beginning of the process it is necessary to keep converging from relatively vague data until the problem is sharply perceived. To do this an individual requires curiosity and skills in perception. But once the problem is perceived, the individual requires an open mind to the collection of facts in order to generate new points of view. The relationship of this to perceptual learning (Chapter 4) will be self-evident. De Bono's lateral thinking approach has excited many teachers in the way that Hudson's research on creativity did some years earlier. Whitfield cites it as a technique for the development of the flexible thinking personality which is required at that stage. But the judgement of the alternatives at the next stage is a convergent activity. The process starts again with the formal definition of the problem (convergent), the generation of novel solutions (divergent), their evaluation and final decision (convergent).

Effective problem solving requires a range of skills for which specific provision needs to be made in learning programmes. Neither should the role of evaluation be under-estimated. The correct solution of a problem, as Clement (1981) shows (see section 5.7) is no guarantee that it is properly understood.

References

J Clement (1981) Solving problems with formulas: some limitations, *Journal of Engineering Education*, 72, 158-62.

E De Bono (1971) *The Use of Lateral Thinking*. Harmondsworth: Penguin.

H I Ellington, E Addinall and F Percival (1981) *Games and Simulations in Science Education*. London: Kogan Page.

W D Furneaux (1962) The psychologist and the university, *Universities Quarterly*, 17, 33-47.

J Heywood (1978) *Examining in Second Level Education*. Dublin: Association of Secondary Teachers, Ireland.

J Heywood and H Montagu-Pollock (1977) *Science for Arts Students: A Case Study in Curriculum Development*. Guildford, Surrey: Society for Research into Higher Education.

K Holt (1977) *Product Innovation*. Sevenoaks, Kent: Newnes-Butterworths.

B Hopson and M Scally (1981) *Life Skills Teaching*. London: McGraw-Hill.

K Jones (1980) *Simulations: A Handbook for Teachers*. London: Kogan Page.

E G Krick (1966) *An Introduction to Engineering Design*. New York: Wiley.

A S Luchins (1942) Mechanisation in problem solving: the effect of 'Einstellung', *Psychological Monographs*, no 248.

F J McDonald (1969) *Educational Psychology*. Belmont, Cal: Wadsworth.

G P Polya (1957) *How to Solve It*. Garden City: Doubleday-Anchor.

W E Red (1981) Problem solving and beginning engineering students, *Journal of Engineering Education*, 72, 169-71.

J Saupé (1961) in P Dressel (ed) *Evaluation in Higher Education*. Boston, Mass: Houghton Mifflin.

P J Tansey (ed) (1971) *Educational Aspects of Simulation*. London: McGraw-Hill.

P R Whitfield (1975) *Creativity in Industry*. Harmondsworth: Penguin.

M Wittrock (1963) Effect of certain sets upon complex verbal learning, *Journal of Educational Psychology*, 54, 85-8.

Note:

Good examples of games designed for schools to develop decision-making skills in pupils are the 'North Sea Exercises' marketed by the Educational Division of British Petroleum.

8 The Curriculum and the Planning and Implementation of Lessons

8.1 Organizing questions

Aims and objectives in the curriculum

1. 'In a post-primary system dominated by public examinations, a teacher who prefers a system approach to teaching and learning understands that he is likely to have to make substantial changes in his approach to teaching.' Discuss.

2. 'Sometimes even one well chosen objective may embrace most of the other aims fundamental to a well-planned course of study, when analysed in detail.' Discuss.

3. Discuss the role of sociology in the 'screening' of aims and objectives in the subject you teach.

4. Discuss the role of either philosophy or psychology in the 'screening' of aims and objectives in the subject you teach.

5. 'When educational objectives are used to define the outcomes of the curriculum, there need be no real conflict between the process and product approaches to curriculum design.' Discuss.

6. 'The new approach links objectives, knowledge and learning experience in such a way that the syllabus is the outcome of the curriculum development process, and assessment an integral part of continuing evaluation.' Critically examine this statement (from Heywood, 1978).

Lesson planning and implementation

7. Distinguish between behavioural and non-behavioural objectives. Give examples of each for a single lesson in the subject you teach. Discuss the advantages and disadvantages of the behavioural objectives approach to the design, implementation and evaluation of studies in the subject you teach.

8. The student teacher was preparing a list of instructional objectives for his history lesson. At this point he was interested in identifying terminal performances. The following three items were part of his list:

(1) The student should demonstrate his genuine understanding of the French Revolution.

(2) The student should be able to name the political leader of the French Revolution.

(3) The student should be able to explain in concrete terms the causes of the Revolution.

Which of the following is the best evaluation of the list?

(a) The list meets all the major requirements of specific statements of instructional objectives.

(b) The list satisfies only one requirement — each statement designates a terminal performance.

(c) The list contains only one statement that adequately describes a terminal performance.

After you have made your choice, give reasons and indicate your basis for rejecting the two other alternatives. (From de Cecco and Crawford, 1974)

9. 'In planning a course a teacher should ask the question, for what purposes and for which students and under what learning conditions should I employ any one method or combination of methods of instruction?' (De Cecco). Discuss. Illustrate, if necessary to your argument, with reference to the subject you teach.

10. An increasing number of curriculum projects publish both learning packages and books together with teacher guides. Briefly, describe any package with which you are familiar. How would you evaluate such packages? What principles of learning would you use in making your judgement?

8.2 The systems approach to curriculum development and design

Our approach to curriculum development and design as well as to the implementation of lessons and their planning is a systems approach. It is illustrated by the diagrams in Chapter 3 (Figures 3.2 and 3.3). It is sometimes called the objectives approach. Although used partially by many authorities, its full implications have seldom been worked out except by research workers. The *Final Report* to the Irish Minister for Education of the Public Examinations Evaluation Project (Heywood, McGuiness and Murphy, 1981) explores the issue in great detail and it is also discussed in Heywood (1978).

The argument of the systems approach is that teachers at any level of education, be it primary, secondary or tertiary, ought to be clear about what they are trying to do, ie about their aims (objectives or goals). No teachers will disagree with this statement, but their interpretation is usually in terms of the syllabus, particularly if they are in secondary or tertiary

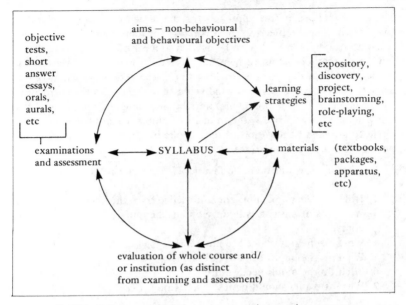

Exhibit 8.1 *A model of the assessment-instruction process*

education. The effect of this combined with much 'chalk and talk' teaching is to emphasize the acquisition of knowledge and its recall at the expense of the higher order skills. Those investigators who defend this point often cite *The Taxonomy of Educational Objectives* (see note at the end of chapter) in their support. The General Studies A level of the General Certificate of Education in England is an attempt to test the different skills in the *Taxonomy*. Other A level examinations also try to test higher level skills than those of comprehension. One investigation in Ireland (MacNamara and Madaus, 1970) demonstrated that the leaving certificate examinations, which are the examinations used for university entry, by and large tested knowledge and comprehension when at that level they ought also to test for application, analysis, and synthesis. The Committee on the Intermediate Certificate, also in Ireland, asked its research unit to try to devise examinations which would test these skills, and confirmed the views that:

1. if higher order skills are to be developed, pupils need to be trained in their performance;
2. because the syllabus and examination dominate teaching so much, the examinations need to be designed to test these skills;
3. the examinations and teaching strategies are therefore intimately related and cannot be divorced from each other;
4. the syllabus will dominate and lead to examinations which have a tendency to test the lower order skills unless tests are specifically designed to test those at the higher levels.

The consequences of this approach for the design of the curriculum are that its aims and objectives have first to be determined. Appropriate teaching strategies have then to be devised to meet these objectives. At the same time methods of assessment appropriate to particular objectives will be developed. In devising the teaching strategies the designer will take into account the concepts, principles and values associated with the curriculum. The syllabus is thus the outcome, not the beginning, of the process. It is not a simple linear process; the model in Exhibit 8.1 has been drawn in a circle to give some indication of its complexity. In devising a syllabus it is necessary to ask such questions as:

1. What change will there be in a pupil's performance at the end of the course?
2. How will the pupil apply the knowledge from this course?
3. What major insight will develop in the pupil as a result of this course?
4. What do the pupils need to know?
5. What do the pupils need to do?
6. What do the pupils need to think?
7. What attitudes should pupils have? (Cone, 1972).

The implications of a system approach for the role of a teacher will now be clear.

8.3 The role of the teacher in curriculum design and evaluation

The role of the teacher according to Tyler is:

☐ to determine the aims and objectives which the curriculum or course should seek to obtain
☐ to select the learning experiences which will help to bring about the attainment of these aims and objectives
☐ to organize those learning experiences so as to provide continuity and sequence for the student and to help him integrate what might otherwise appear as isolated experiences
☐ to determine the extent to which these aims and objectives are being attained.

The teacher's roles in discipline and motivation relate to the efficiency of learning which in turn relate to the attainment of aims and objectives.

8.4 Terminology: the problem of the curriculum

Many statements have been made about what the total process of education should achieve. More often than not they include value positions which require a particular set of attitudes, skills and knowledge to be developed by the pupils.

Whatever we may think of such statements, it can seldom be said that their goals are attained. In secondary and tertiary education the emphasis is on the subject, which detracts from the systematic discussion of values and value positions. In this sense higher education is not liberal. However, in some of the liberal arts colleges (eg Alverno College) in the United States systematic attempts to develop teaching strategies for the study of values have been made.

At second level, the syllabus objectives of examinations often include value positions. However, questions which will cause students to discuss values are seldom incorporated. In consequence the pupils do not rate them as important since they do not expect to be examined in them. This is not to say that teachers do not see their importance or try to do something about it: the response below shows much dedication to this point. Teachers of English in particular see this as part of their role (see also p 105 and Exhibit 8.7). One of the respondents wrote:

> The different levels of cognitive development suggested by Bloom — knowledge, comprehension, application, analysis, synthesis, and evaluation — are a useful means of checking whether or not we have dealt with all the levels of development we intended to. Knowledge may underpin all the categories, but our English teacher's objective cannot be covered simply by making sure pupils know how to spell and punctuate, and know who says what and when in the novel or play.
>
> If we want our pupils to develop personally, then we must attempt to give them the means whereby they can comprehend what others say to them, we want to attempt to give them the means to use their knowledge of language to present themselves to others, to analyse and bring together the strands of their experience, and finally make judgements which will be the basis of decisions and actions in the future. Research suggests that a lot of this sort of development is the function of the *maturation* process and would happen inevitably anyway. Because of this a general education such as this in late adolescence has very little value. However, by recognizing that these developments are taking place, a teacher can perhaps facilitate their development and give opportunities for experience that might not exist in another situation. This involves many of the categories of Bloom's affective domain — receiving, responding, valuing, organizing, and characterizing — which again should be recognized by the teacher. In this particular instance the interconnection of the affective and cognitive domains needs to be recognized and skilful handling of the cognitive areas by the teacher can deal with the affective domain too without introducing it explicitly. How can we, in any case, teach someone to value anything abstract? If we discuss a text on racialism, looking at what is said and how it is said, analysing the various arguments and keeping them separate from our own opinions (one of the most difficult things for children to do in my experience) then perhaps our pupils will end up valuing particular attitudes. Of course the question of what we want them to value arises here and illustrates the problems inherent in the affective domain. Do we teach/transmit

our own values, and if so, what right have we to do so?

In conclusion, while one well chosen objective may indeed embrace most of the other aims fundamental to a well planned course of study, and will serve to clarify the teacher's ideas and focus his attention, it is necessary that the sub-units, the underlying aims and objectives, should also be formulated if the teacher is to carry out an effective programme. This is probably best done by testing these aims against the various levels of Bloom's *Taxonomy*, so ensuring or at least giving the opportunity to promote all the desired skills.

8.5 Terminology: the terms themselves

(a) Organizing responses

There is much terminological confusion abounding at the present moment. This may be due to the fact that British educators seemed more concerned with stating aims than objectives and American educators are more concerned with objectives.

Both aims and objectives refer to educational intention and purpose but they vary in their degrees of specificity and generality.

I would like to take an aim as referring to the overall view I have of modern languages:

1. to develop awareness of another culture;
2. to develop an understanding of language as a system of communication;
3. to contribute to the child's social and moral development.

A behaviour I would see as being more specific; the degree of specificity depending on the type:

(a) non-behavioural objective: what you intend to do in the whole class, eg to further the class's understanding of *Le Tac* by Alphonse de Famartre;
(b) behavioural objective: what one class will be able to perform; eg at the end of a 45-minute lesson on *Le Tac* by Alphonse de Famartre the class will be able to:
   (i) outline the various images used for time;
  (ii) name the metre;
 (iii) suggest whether the poem is pessimistic or optimistic;
 (iv) say when it was written.

For example, a course in hygiene might have as its objective 'to motivate people to keep themselves clean'. This would include a lot of lesser objectives, the objectives of each lesson, eg:

1. to demonstrate how diseases spread;
2. to show the importance of proper sanitation;
3. to demonstrate the causes of teeth decay.

My class consisted of first-year boys and girls and my job was to teach them Irish. At first I set out my objectives which were very similar in structure to the objectives of any language lecture. For example:

1. that the pupils should be able to understand, write and use verbs in various tenses;
2. that the pupils should understand a certain amount of basic grammar necessary in order to complete a sentence;
3. that the pupils should be able to understand how to plan out an essay in Irish and then to write one.

I set out with these objectives and many more carefully laid out but I soon found that my objectives were becoming entangled. I didn't seem to be achieving any worthwhile results. Each objective became as unclear to me as it did to the pupils. I decided then to choose one main objective and this was that the students would be able to have a fair competence in the Irish language, both in written and in oral form. I based my objective on the notional/functional of teaching a language.

(b) Commentary

The terms which a particular curriculum designer will use are also the cause of much confusion. They can unwittingly cause emotional reactions. One such term is 'skill'. In this context it means 'learning skill': for example 'the ability to make relevant hypotheses'. Unfortunately in Britain and Ireland skill is associated with the use of tools, and since practical abilities are not by and large highly valued in those societies the use of the term skill unless prefixed by learning is likely to turn teachers off.

Similarly the idea that learning is a behaviour is also found to be objectionable. Teachers fail to realize that they themselves want to change pupil behaviour; when a person learns something, he undergoes a change in behaviour. If we can state precisely what it is we expect a person to do at the end of a particular learning session, we are therefore stating a *behavioural objective*, and we can state these for any activity on the curriculum. Of course, certain propositions are more complex than others; a naive approach to curriculum design and evaluation is not possible. Nor is it possible, as was emphasized at the end of Chapter 7, to provide a ready made matrix which teachers can use.

We can therefore distinguish four levels of educational planning:

1. the total curriculum
2. the subject
3. the course within a subject
4. the individual lesson.

For each of these it is possible to distinguish aims, non-behavioural objectives and behavioural objectives. They represent different levels of focusing on a problem area or topic. Similarly each of the levels above is of increasing specificity. We can distinguish between behavioural and non-behavioural objectives by the instructional verb used at the beginning of the statement. A behavioural statement is always an action statement (eg the pupil will be able to write, design, diagnose, analyse, select, identify, apply, etc). In contrast, terms like know, understand, appreciate are non-behavioural. This is not to say that they are unnecessary in the process of lesson focusing. The second organizing response is dealing with aims and non-behavioural objectives in this terminology — not non-behavioural objectives. The same applies to the third response. Exhibit 8.2, which should be self-explanatory, illustrates these points for an individual lesson. Exhibit 8.3 relates a student's experience of using this method over four lessons. In a single lesson plan the non-behavioural objectives would be stated more precisely than in the Exhibit. Exhibit 8.4 shows the objectives for the *Place, Time and Society* course (Blyth *et al*, 1975) for which the key concepts were given in the last chapter.

8.6 Selecting aims and objectives at the level of the subject and the curriculum

My advocacy of the systems approach arose from work on examinations (see Chapter 7 and above). I was concerned to focus on a few significant objectives around which sub-tests within an examination paper could be designed. Broad skills were called on such as those of comprehension, planning, evaluation. The questions focused on those within the framework of the subject being examined. Clearly many other skills (abilities, qualities) were tested. The sub-tests focused on an activity thought to be important in the process of being an engineer, or a historian or a mathematician. This required statements of aims and objectives. Several examining authorities state aims and objectives in this way but not all of them set specific sub-tests to see whether they are attained; nor do all of them separate behavioural from non-behavioural objectives, aims from objectives, or the cognitive from the affective domain. In fact, this does not seem to be necessary. The statement of aims for the Irish Intermediate Certificate Examination in History (see Exhibit 4.2) is an example of this mix. Nevertheless, it is clear that it provides sufficient focus for the development of a multi-strategy examination (Heywood, McGuinness and Murphy, 1981). My opinion of the student response in Exhibit 8.5 is that contrary to that student's opinion, her description could be translated into the terms of *The Taxonomy of Educational Objectives*. However, at the same time, I do not feel this to be necessary. We should always follow the approach which interests us provided that we can evaluate what we do with some objectivity. Previous chapters have shown how difficult this is.

Lecturer:

Class: Kitchen Groups 1 & 2

Subject: Catering Science and Technology

Date:

Time: 2 hours

AIM

To instruct in the operation, use and limitations of the microwave oven.

NON-BEHAVIOURAL OBJECTIVES

To create an understanding of the principles of microwave heating, which will enable safe and efficient use of a microwave oven.

BEHAVIOURAL OBJECTIVES

The student will be able to:

1. identify which cooking processes can be carried out in different types of microwave ovens, and which cannot

2. select the most appropriate microwave oven to purchase for any given operation

3. identify those containers which may or may not be used in a microwave oven.

4. operate and maintain a microwave oven in a safe and efficient way.

5. obtain the best possible results from heating/cooking in it.

Exhibit 8.2

For four lessons:

I set out my aims which were to give the children an insight into the Tudor kings, queens and their lifestyles. This was to cover a few lessons beginning with Henry VII.

I set out my behavioural and non-behavioural objectives, for example:

NON-BEHAVIOURAL OBJECTIVES

1. To make the children aware of the innovations brought about in England by Henry VII.

2. To give the children an opportunity of observing the work of a great man taking into account the need for authority, rules and regulations, loyalty.

BEHAVIOURAL OBJECTIVES

1. To describe how Henry VII came to the throne.

2. To discuss the character of Henry VII.

3. To compare and contrast the character of Henry VII with other Tudor monarchs.

Exhibit 8.3

	Skills			Personal qualities
	Intellectual	Social	Physical	Interests, attitudes, values
	1. The ability to find information from a variety of sources, in a variety of ways 2. The ability to communicate findings through an appropriate medium 3. The ability to interpret pictures, charts, graphs, maps, etc 4. The ability to evaluate information 5. The ability to organize information through concepts and generalizations 6. The ability to formulate and test hypotheses and generalizations	1. The ability to participate within small groups 2. An awareness of significant groups within the community and the wider society 3. A developing understanding of how individuals relate to such groups 4. A willingness to consider participating constructively in the activities associated with these groups 5. The ability to exercise empathy (ie the capacity to imagine accurately what it might be like to be someone else)	1. The ability to manipulate equipment 2. The ability to manipulate equipment to find and communicate information 3. The ability to explore the expressive powers of the human body to communicate ideas and feelings 4. The ability to plan and execute expressive activities to communicate ideas and feelings	1. The fostering of curiosity through the encouragement of questions 2. The fostering of a wariness of overcommitment to one framework of explanation and the possible distortion of facts and the omission of evidence 3. The fostering of a willingness to explore personal attitudes and values to relate these to other people's 4. The encouraging of an openness to the possibility of change in attitudes and values 5. The encouragement of worthwhile and developing interests in human affairs

Exhibit 8.4 *An example of the curriculum objectives of the* Place, Time and Society *course developed in the School of Education of the University of Liverpool.* (Blyth *et al*, 1975; reproduced by kind permission of the authors.)

8.7 Screening

One problem for the curriculum designer is that while it is true that many use *The Taxonomy of Educational Objectives* there are numerous sources of aims and objectives. The *Taxonomy* is specifically behavioural and may be applied to any curriculum once its aims have been determined. But an alternative approach would be to apply Gagné's list of learning outcomes, which are equally behavioural, and are shown in Exhibit 8.6. My colleagues and I (Youngman *et al*, 1978) have been analysing the jobs actually done by individuals to derive educational and training objectives based on the jobs done by people at work. Others have used the model of a scientist at work (Furst, 1960).

At the level of the curriculum there are many aims and objectives. Some can be contradictory, in which case they are not likely to be attained. The curriculum designer is concerned with selecting a few significant aims and objectives on which to focus the curriculum design, a process which is sometimes called 'screening'.

The curriculum designer should draw on the disciplines of the philosophy, sociology and psychology of education. The former two are very much about values and education's relation to society, while the latter has more to do with learning. The idea of using these disciplines is more easily grasped from the learning aspect. If, for example, we believe Piaget's theory to be correct, we are likely to object to the teaching of abstract concepts before the age of 13 or 14 on the ground that the pupils will not have reached an appropriate stage of cognitive development. One student drew attention to the value of Kohlberg's theory of moral development (see p 24) in helping the teacher of religious education to formulate aims. Her argument for Kohlberg concludes in this way:

> In the first place, he suggests, *à la* Piaget, several tests that could be given to a class, to get an idea of their entering behaviour. That is, they assess the level of moral development of each child.
>
> Secondly, once this is done, the teacher will have an idea of what sequence to follow. She is given an orderly sequence. She knows how to try to probe each child at a level just beyond his present level. She knows that the presentation of material at an earlier level, or at a much later level, will bore and/or confuse him.
>
> Thirdly, referring back to the first point, she is provided with a standard of assessment. Is the child at the same level at the end of the year? Has any development occurred?
>
> Kohlberg's theories thus provide the RE teacher with a very useful structure by which to screen aims and objectives. A teacher with the general aim 'to make students more moral' can — through Kohlberg — 'screen' these into specific objectives.

While I would not agree wholly with the approach of the response below in answer to a question on the use of sociology in screening, the student does show how considerations of the received and reflexive views of

'The aims and objectives of this particular course are not stated in terms which show a clear relationship to Bloom's *Taxonomy*, neither do they quite reflect a process model based on a musician's way of working; rather, being a general course, the aims and objectives set out in the content of the syllabus (rather than in the introduction) resemble a process model — if one could so describe it — of a well-informed member of a concert audience. The main emphasis central to the objectives is on the ability to listen to music intelligently, and the examination itself clearly reflects this, since it is primarily an aural examination, with written questions added.

One particular, well-chosen objective, which I should like to analyse, is the ability to differentiate between musical styles (tested by comparison of contrasting short extracts). This, I feel, embraces most of the course's other aims, because it represents a synthesis of various objectives which must be achieved separately first, and gradually combined. One of the aims implied in the differentiation of musical styles is the appreciation of certain characteristics of any one style — a judgement of the general atmosphere, colouring and apparent message of a piece of music which is unfamiliar. This aim needs to be supplemented by a general appreciation of shape, form and structure in any musical context.

These two aims can then be further broken down to reach specific objectives, such as: historical knowledge of instrumentation used (which in turn depends on the ability to recognize the sounds of different vocal combinations or musical instruments), and of conventions of form; appreciation of structure in turn depends on experience of tonal and rhythmic patterns, which at the earliest stages of the course should have been internalized through practical experience. The characteristics of individual composers' writing within a similar historical period may need to be appreciated only in a general way at this stage; but that again depends on a background knowledge of specific features, which in turn relies on experience of elements of harmony, etc, which is best achieved by practical skill, and by listening to (and/or singing or playing) specific examples of music in differing styles. To accommodate this last, certain musical works are set for analytical study in the syllabus, and 30 songs of varied style and origin are set to be learned and examined for form, small-scale features of style, etc.'

Exhibit 8.5

Type of learning outcome	Principles of planning learning
Motor skills	For example, soldering, changing gear when driving. Establish those components of the skill which are of critical significance. Practice these intensively and then, equally intensively, the total skill.
Verbal information	An individual fact or item should be accompanied by some meaningful context. In the Gagné model of learning the order of sequence of major sub-topics is not of importance.
Intellectual skills	Instructions on how each new skill should be learned should be given prior to the learning of the new skill. Subordinate skills should be mastered first. Only then should the learning context for the new major skill be provided.
Attitudes	Attitude situations involve the learner in making choices. Information relevant to the choices to be made must be learned first. Skills in making choices must be mastered. The learner must respect the source. (See p 74 for a discussion of the problem of dissonance.)
Cognitive strategies	Information which is necessary for the solution of a problem should be learned first. The problem will be designed to utilize intellectual skills which have already been acquired.

Exhibit 8.6 *Gagné's list of learning outcomes*

Note: The above table illustrates a development by Gagné and Briggs (1974) of Gagné's idea of a sequence of instruction in which the lower steps of the hierarchy must be mastered before the higher steps can be learned. It relates in particular to the planning and sequencing of lessons and/or the curriculum. In this approach none of the steps can be circumvented. However, the learning outcomes are not arranged in hierarchical order in this application. It is an extreme illustration of the application that for learning to be effective it must have meaning, organization and structure. Some of our students have found the general ideas presented by Gagné of considerable value although they made their own empirical adaptations (see, for example, p 116).

knowledge can influence a teacher (see p 33). It seems to me that the inclusion of the 'ability to think critically' must be acceptable even within the framework of a received criticism. Precisely because society accepts critical thinking as an objective, we should both allow for and accept change of the kind described by the restructuring perspective. Nevertheless, the response which follows shows the significance of sociology in screening.

The 'received' perspective sees the nature of knowledge as something 'given' — knowledge is absolute and hence what society accepts as 'normal knowledge' is what should be transmitted to children. Related to this given knowledge are given norms and values, also defined by society. This view of knowledge sees it as closely related to power — those with the control of knowledge, its content, distribution and evaluation, are those in positions of power, and hence concerned with the legitimation of the knowledge and the preservation of the status quo. If one accepts this view, then is there a place for the teaching of critical thinking skills in society? The answer would appear to be 'no'. The economy in a modern society is one of the chief determinants of who will have power. If the present economic structures are threatened (which they might be if critically evaluated) then those in positions of power are also threatened.

The opposite view to the 'received' one is the 'reflexive' one. While the received perspective has its roots in philosophy ('essences' and 'ideal forms') and psychology (fixed structures thought — Piaget's 'stages' in cognitive development) the reflexive view is based mainly on sociological theories. It sees knowledge as being relative to individual perceptions — there is no absolute reality. Berger and Luckman's views of the 'social construct of reality' is an articulation of this view. The perspective is also based on phenomenological analysis — consciousness is subjective, when we perceive something we bestow a meaning on it, which will depend on our subjective consciousness, which has been determined by our past experiences. Thus, knowledge is not something to be brought into the classroom by a teacher in neat and fixed packages, but is something which is determined in the classroom, by the perceptions of the individuals therein.

In this view the development of critical thinking skills would be a desirable one. The economic structure is as it is only because it has been defined by those in power. It is something which can be questioned and therefore changed, and for this to happen critical evaluation will be necessary.

A third possible view would be a Marxist one, viewing society in terms of conflict. This perspective would certainly be amicable towards the development of critical thinking skills.

However, at this stage one must probe more deeply into how society actually works. Even if one takes the second viewpoint, is the aim of teaching critical thinking skills feasible? Those holding a 'received' perspective are generally those in the positions of control. Can the sanctions which act to prevent 'reflexivity' be overcome — sanctions which may not only be imposed by society, but by one's pupils who, in one view, have been indoctrinated into the norms of society through the 'hidden' curriculum as well as the formal one? Economics, a social science, would appear to provide many opportunities for the promotion of critical thinking skills. However, in the past year I have found that attempts to introduce an element of questioning into teaching economics, a presentation of alternative viewpoints, have been met by a request to say which is 'right', ie which will be acceptable in the exam. To develop critical thinking skills, more than just teaching strategies will need to be considered. The whole hidden curriculum which has bred acceptance in children will need to be restructured. This is a slow process, severely handicapped by the insistent demands springing from exams.

8.8 Focusing on a single well-chosen aim

Behind question 2 at the beginning of this chapter is the idea that if an aim can provide a focus the objectives will follow. An example would be 'to provide an understanding of the way in which a scientist solves problems'. The implication is that the teacher will have to decide what skills the scientist uses in solving problems (see Exhibit 7.1). The danger is that it will lead the teacher simply to concentrate on the syllabus.

Exhibit 8.7 (another student response) shows how the course can be broken down into objectives. It is easy to imagine this student's lessons structured by objectives of one kind or another. It is difficult to believe the same thing of the example in Exhibit 8.8 (also a student response), but this may be unfair: it does not mean that lesson objectives could not necessarily be derived from this student's aims. The primary idea should provide a stimulus to the planning of a course. Given this, the question is whether the objectives approach is of value in lesson planning.

8.9 The objectives approach in lesson planning

An example of this in a language class would be to tell the child that by the end of the class he will be able to use the concept of masculine and feminine — *le* and *la* in French. It is important that the child knows in which direction he is travelling or he will become inattentive.

Throughout the discussion of learning in the preceding chapters it has been demonstrated that lessons need adequate planning. This planning has to take into account motivation, as well as the way in which pupils acquire concepts and principles, and learn to solve problems. Among the principles of learning which were enunciated were that:

☐ Learning proceeds much more rapidly and is retained much longer when that which has to be learned possesses meaning, organization and structure

'I take from my own experience the example of teaching a fifth-year class of 16+ girls for English. The text being used was George Orwell's *1984*. I set the general aim of "Reading the book critically".
Achievement of this objective involved planning a learning strategy towards helping the girls develop and use the skills necessary to read critically; evaluation by questioning and homework exercises provided feedback to me and to the pupils to enable us to modify our technique as necessary.

Simple understanding of the narrative and plot involved the skill of *comprehension*. This was easily checked by questioning. Picking out the significant elements in the story and connecting them to make a coherent pattern involved using *analytic* and *synthesizing* skills. Thus, the overall pattern of the totalitarian society was identified by bringing together the threads of Thought Police, Newspeak, Doublethink, etc. *Extrapolation* of the events and scenes in the book to contemporary times led on to the process of *evaluation*. The girls were required to consider not just whether the story was convincing but the role of propaganda and whether in fact the *book itself* was a piece of propaganda.

Towards the achievement of this general aim, the learning strategy concentrated on directing the students' minds to the text itself for evidence to support any assertion they might make. The questioning in class moved from the lower order 'what' and 'where' questions to the higher order ones of 'why'. Emphasis was placed on pupil-pupil interaction with me as a catalyst. This was done through getting a different student to produce a short essay for each class period, and having the class discuss it. The content of the essay was determined by me and thus I exercised control over the learning experience for that class period.'

Exhibit 8.7

'A general objective for the year may be planned and presented to the class, eg "this year (or term) we shall be studying everyday life in France. We shall be discovering how and where the French live, how they go shopping, how they go to work and what type of work they do, what they do at weekends and during the holidays, etc."

This single objective covers a vast range of material: vocabulary dealing with houses, flats, shops and shopping, travel, work, sport, leisure, hobbies; grammar presenting new verbs, syntax, adjectives. The objective is clear: after stating the objective, the teacher should add what the class will achieve by the end of the year/term: "so at the end of this year/term, you will be able to describe where you live in French, what you do at the weekends and during the holidays, what hobbies you have. You will know a lot more about French life and, if you go to France, you will be able to talk about your home, your interests; you will be able to go shopping and order food in a café or restaurant." '

Exhibit 8.8

Class: . . . .

Ability range: . . . .

Aids required: . . . .

Aim	Lesson phases	Content	Learning strategies
	Introduction		eg
Non-behavioural objective	Presentation	Facts	Large group Small group Individualized
Behavioural objective	Application	Concepts	Discovery Guided discovery Expository
		Principles	Role playing Case study Project work Laboratory work
(Problem to be solved)	Conclusion	(Problem to be solved)	
Questioning			

Exhibit 8.9 *Scheme for a lesson plan*

☐ Transfer can only occur when there is a recognized similarity between the learning situation and the transfer situation.

The response above shows how, by stating the objectives at the beginning of the lesson in terms of behaviour, the pupil is made aware of the purpose of the lesson and of what is expected of him. The advantages to both the pupil and the teacher should be clear:

1. both sides to the learning contract have an objective which they understand;
2. statements by the teacher of what is expected of the pupils at the end of the lesson will ensure that its objectives are attained;
3. inspection of these statements will readily indicate to the teacher whether too much is expected of the pupils;
4. they are especially useful in remedial work (see Ainscow and Tweddle, 1979).

In general teachers seem to want to cram too much into a lesson. An awareness of the problems pupils face in learning, re-interpreted in a statement of objectives, should provide a realistic approach to lesson planning.

Lesson plans can be derived from a scheme. This scheme will include subject name; number of lessons; and particulars of the children (age; sex; ability; number). A statement of aim or content will accompany each lesson. Notes will be made on the way in which class will be organized, the equipment which will be used, and the way the course will be assessed. Subsequently non-behavioural objectives are derived from the aims for each lesson, and the behavioural objectives can be stated.

However, as was shown in Chapter 3 each lesson has to be developed to maintain motivation. Notes can be drawn up in terms of Gagné's learning sequence, ie motivation, apprehension (attending, perceiving, comprehending), acquisition, retention, recall, generalization, performance and feedback. Following Cohen and Garner (1971), these may be reduced to four stages, ie introduction, presentation, application and conclusion. Lesson notes showing content in one column and method in another can be drawn up. Cohen and Mannion (1977) give several detailed examples of this approach. Student teachers ought to go into this amount of detail in their initial training. One reservation about these examples is that they do not always highlight concepts and principles.

There are many ways of approaching the design of lessons. For example, Gagné also gives examples of lesson plans derived from his learning theory. Whatever approach is used, the very minimum for lesson planning is a statement of aim, non-behavioural objective, and behavioural objective in the style of Exhibit 8.2. An outline scheme for the overall activity of lesson planning is shown in Exhibit 8.9. It is clear that the greater a teacher understanding of the applied psychology of instruction the more likely his plan is to lead to effective teaching.

This chapter concludes with a curriculum outline in geography completed by a student as part of course work assessment in that subject.

A STUDENT TEACHER'S EXAMPLE OF A GEOGRAPHY CURRICULUM FOR 12-15-YEAR-OLDS
Gina Plunkett

Year 1

Objectives	Key Concepts	Specific Content	Learning Experiences
1. To develop the specific geographic skills of observation and exploration 2. To find information from the local environment 3. To analyse, synthesize and evaluate the information which has been uncovered 4. To map and survey areas 5. To appreciate the wealth and value of the home environment 6. To work co-operatively in groups	ENVIRONMENT (similarity and differences)	1. School and home: (a) location (b) scale (c) situation (d) distance (i) location and distance in relation to Dublin, Bray and Dun Laoghaire (ii) location and distance in relation to childrens' homes (iii) study of the nearest centre (Ballybrack) looking at: (a) old and new (b) functions (c) benefits and drawbacks	*Plans:* Making plans of school and home *Field trips:* These trips would include exercises in mapping, land use surveys, classification of shops etc. Collection of information on the age, structure and appearance of significant buildings *Group work:* The class would then be divided into groups to organize and process the collected data. Groups would work on specific topics. The end result would be the compilation of a geographic study of the local environment
1. To apply what they have learned in previous lessons to new situations 2. To formulate generalizations 3. To develop a sense of perspective 4. To evaluate the effects of urbanization 5. To analyse information presented in map form	URBANIZATION (continuity and change)	1. The local environment (Ballybrack) as part of the city of Dublin 2. The growth and spread of Dublin over time: (a) population changes (b) location of housing (c) functions 3. Potential for future growth and problems envisaged	*Problem solving:* The students will be presented with information on the development of Dublin into a large urban area *Simulation model:* 21st century Dublin. Given what they (the students) know about the situation and if they were planners where would they:

GEOGRAPHY CURRICULUM (12-15-year-olds)

Year 1 (continued)

Objectives	Key Concepts	Specific Content	Learning Experiences
		4. Dublin in relation to other urban centres in Ireland	(a) locate new industry (b) locate new housing estates (c) locate new roads? *Map:* Construct a map based on population size showing the relative importance of Dublin to other centres
1. To map space in alternatives to real linear scale terms 2. To evaluate alternatives 3. To realize the importance of transport networks	COMMUNICATIONS (cause and consequences)	1. Links between Dublin and other urban centres: (a) road network (b) rail network 2. Purpose of these links: (a) trade (b) transport (c) accessibility	*Map:* Topological map showing connections between centres *Map transformation:* Time distance map from Dublin to selected centres outside Dublin *Problem:* To evaluate the present major national transport networks *Role-playing:* The students pretend they are businessmen engaged in the distribution of goods. Given haulage costs, commodity type and distances, what mode of transport would they use for transporting goods, when considering (a) time costs (b) mileage costs?

GEOGRAPHY CURRICULUM (12-15-year-olds)

Year 1 (continued)

Objectives	Key Concepts	Specific Content	Learning Experiences
1. To appreciate the land as a valuable but limited resource 2. To make and test hypotheses 3. To manage equipment 4. To represent distributions using maps 5. To understand the connection between soil and natural and cultivated vegetation 6. To realize the potential of rivers 7. To appreciate the wealth of the sea 8. To interpret charts and graphs	RESOURCES (use and abuse)	1. Land: (a) soil (b) natural vegetation (c) cultivated vegetation (d) power – turf 2. Rivers: (a) power – HEP (b) water supply 3. Sea and lakes: (a) fishing industry 4. Weather and climate: (a) regional differences	*Field trips:* Collect data on local soil vegetation types *Classroom experiments:* Setting up simple experiments to test soil types, soil structure, etc *Group work:* Draw map showing the distribution of soil types in the local area. Draw map showing vegetation types *Map:* Showing distribution of HEP stations in Ireland *Map:* Showing location of fish types and fishing ports in Ireland. Interpretation and construction of charts, graphs and meteorological maps
1. To see the connection between various geomorphological processes and resultant forms 2. To understand the landscape without man 3. To draw sketches of landforms 4. To recognize landforms on maps	LANDFORMS (process and form)	1. Rocks 2. Weathering 3. Erosion – running water 4. Deposition – running water	*Field work:* Day trip to Glencree (observation) *Map:* Using a geological map of Ireland and a map showing the major mountain ranges, construct a map showing the location of the

GEOGRAPHY CURRICULUM (12-15-year-olds)

Year 1 (continued)

Objectives	Key Concepts	Specific Content	Learning Experiences
			mountains and their rock type. Photographs could be used to illustrate the influence of rock type on mountain form

Year 2

Objectives	Key Concepts	Specific Content	Learning Experiences
1. To understand environments other than their own 2. To project themselves into the way of life of other societies and cultures 3. To appreciate the values and ways of other cultures 4. To collect meaningful information and to communicate it through an appropriate medium	ENVIRONMENT (similarity and difference)	1. Great Britain: (a) location and distance in relation to Ireland (b) characteristics in common with Ireland; characteristics which differ from Ireland 2. Europe (the EEC): (a) locations and distances in relation to Ireland (b) characteristics in common with Ireland; characteristics which differ from Ireland	*Data collection:* Students would collect information on the cultural, social and physical environment of Great Britain. Pictorial information would be included on wall charts. The main theme would be similarity and difference. Emphasis could be on: (1) language (2) lifestyles (3) landscapes. Articles would then be written evaluating what students had learned about Great Britain *Group work:* Groups would be organized, and each group would deal with one EEC country in a similar approach to that used for Great Britain

Year 2 (continued)

GEOGRAPHY CURRICULUM (12-15-year-olds)

Objectives	Key Concepts	Specific Content	Learning Experiences
1. To understand the effect of time on the environment 2. To appreciate both city and country life 3. To apply models and theories to real life situations	URBANIZATION (continuity and change)	1. Urbanization in Great Britain (historical development) 2. Cause of city growth: (a) industrial revolution (b) demographic factors 3. Consequence of city growth: (a) conurbation-metropolis 4. Settlement patterns: (a) hierarchies (b) centrality 5. Urban functions (a) functional zones	*Map work:* 1. Maps of British Isles showing the growth of cities over time 2. Map showing the distribution of raw materials and industrial cities Application of Christaler's model Application of Burgess' model
1. To perceive space more accurately 2. To understand the utilization of space 3. To understand social interaction in spatial terms 4. To keep records	COMMUNICATION (cause and consequence)	1. Travel – interaction patterns: (a) journey to school, shops, visiting (b) journey for holidays 2. Holidays: (a) at home (b) abroad 3. Airports – travel and trade 4. Seaports – travel and trade 5. Markets: (a) function (b) location	*Class survey:* Interaction study: Each student would record each journey he made from his home to his destination for a whole week. In class he would then plot this data on a map. The pattern which emerges would be explained in terms of node edges, distance *Map work:* Maps showing the students' preferences for holiday places at home and abroad *Maps:* Showing trade routes: analysis of maps

GEOGRAPHY CURRICULUM (12-15-year-olds)

Year 2 (continued)

Objectives	Key Concepts	Specific Content	Learning Experiences

1. To understand that resources are limited and should therefore be used efficiently and sparingly	RESOURCES (use and abuse)	*Land:*
		1. Power:
		  (a) oil
		  (b) coal
			Field trip:
			Farm survey and interview with farmer

2. To understand the way of life of different types of farmers in Ireland and the world		2. Forestry
		3. Farming practices:
		  (a) biosphere
		  (b) economic sphere	

3. To appreciate the work of the farmer		4. Competition for land: (a) rural – urban interaction	Application of Von Thunen model
4. To realize the value of land in economic and aesthetic terms		(b) reclamation 5. Tourism	
5. To understand the delicate ecological balance between man and nature			

1. To discriminate meaningful information on maps	LANDFORMS (process and form)	1. Ice:
		  (a) ice ages
		  (b) structure of glaciers
			Map work:
			Interpretation of landforms on maps

2. To apply knowledge about landform development to information on map		(c) work of glaciers (d) present day glaciers	*Photographs:* Interpretation of landforms on aerial photographs and oblique photographs

3. To interpret and analyse photographs		2. Earth movements
		3. Tropical landscapes:
		  (a) processes
		  (b) forms	

4. To distinguish between features found in Ireland and those found in different climatic regions		4. Desert landscapes:
		  (a) processes
		  (b) forms	

5. To understand the age of the earth and the processes at work which have shaped it and continue to give shape to it			

159

GEOGRAPHY CURRICULUM (12-15-year-olds)

Year 3

Objectives	Key Concepts	Specific Content	Learning Experiences
1. The fostering of willingness to explore personal attitudes and values and to relate these to other people	ENVIRONMENTS (similarity and difference)	1. Tropical lands 2. Temperate lands 3. Cold lands	*Group work:* Various groups make a study of these three environments. Work could be divided into: (a) physical environments (b) social environments (c) cultural environments (d) overview
2. To understand how other peoples interact with their particular environments			
3. To make connections between concepts and percepts which have been learned in previous lessons to the present analyses			
4. The encouraging of an openness to the possibility of change in attitudes and values			
1. To develop in the students an ability to plan	URBANIZATION (continuity and change)	1. Urbanization on a global scale: (a) process over time (b) third world cities (problems of growth)	Application of Rostow's stages of development
2. To apply theories to new situations and to evaluate the result		2. Economic development: (a) agriculture to industry (b) stages of development and the third world (c) theories — growth centres v decentralization	Evaluation of theories
3. To develop and test hypotheses		3. Planning city growth: (a) urban sprawl and decay (b) renovation and renewal (c) rehousing and new towns	*Group project:* 1. Field work around Dublin collecting information 2. Classwork: an urban study of Dublin emphasizing the problems
4. To work in a group and to co-ordinate efforts and delegate tasks			

GEOGRAPHY CURRICULUM (12-15-year-olds)

Year 3 (continued)

Objectives	Key Concepts	Specific Content	Learning Experiences
1. The ability to represent and interpret movement patterns on maps 2. To understand the way of life of a migrant 3. To understand the causes and consequences of the many forms of communication	COMMUNICATIONS (cause and consequences)	4. Shannon development 5. Dublin 1. Migration: (a) over time – case study USA (b) present migrations (c) reasons for migration (d) effects of migration 2. Irish Railway Development: (a) growth and decline (b) plans for the future 3. Development of ports: (a) general development (b) case study of Dublin and Waterford	associated with growth and proposing possible solutions. *Map:* Showing wave of immigrants to USA Various maps showing stages of railway development and decline. Suggest reasons for decline
1. To appreciate the need for conservation 2. To understand how man can upset the ecosystem 3. The ability to use photographs as a means of analysis	RESOURCES (use and abuse)	1. Alternative energy 2. Pollution: (a) land (b) water (c) air 3. Polluted lakes and rivers in Ireland 4. Depletion of fish stocks	*Photographs:* Looking at the effects of various types of pollution, suggesting causes and proposing possible methods of preventing pollution

GEOGRAPHY CURRICULUM (12-15-year-olds)

Year 3 (continued)

Objectives	Key Concepts	Specific Content	Learning Experiences

1. To encourage an understanding of man/land interaction
2. To appreciate the damage which man can do to his environment
3. To understand how man can upset geomorphological systems
4. To understand the time lag which may exist between cause and effect
	LANDFORMS (process and form)	1. Coastal erosion:
		  (a) causes
		  (b) prevention and cure
		2. Wind erosion:
		  (a) causes
		  (b) prevention and cure
		3. River erosion:
		  (a) causes
		  (b) prevention and cure
			Time maps of coastal areas showing evolution of coastlines

A note on *The Taxonomy of Educational Objectives*

In 1948 a group of American psychologists began to search for a common terminology for describing and referring to the human behavioural characteristics which were tested in schools and colleges. It emerged as a set of behavioural objectives which describe 'the thoughts students are expected to develop as a result of the instructional process'. Tests for objectives in both the cognitive and affective domains were described in two volumes. These were:

B Bloom (ed) (1964) *The Taxonomy of Educational Objectives, Vol 1: Cognitive Domain*. London: Longmans Green.

D Krathwohl (ed) (1964) *The Taxonomy of Educational Objectives, Vol 2: Affective Domain*. London: Longmans Green.

The basic classification is as follows:

Knowledge (recall) of:
specifics
terminology
specific facts
ways and means of dealing with specifics
conventions
trends and sequences
classifications and categories
criteria
methodology
universals and abstractions in a field
principles and generalizations
theories and structures

Behavioural objectives
(learning skills)
comprehension
application
analysis
synthesis
judgement (evaluation)

These skills are ranked hierarchically. In this scheme knowledge is basic, and is that which we recall. Before any problem-solving activity can begin, there must be comprehension. In many examination papers there is a passage against which questions are set to test that it is comprehended. Within comprehension there are sub-objectives of translation, interpretation and extrapolation. The other categories are treated similarly. At the operational level, all the skills in Exhibit 7.2 are to be found in the detailed categorization of the *Taxonomy*.

As indicated in the text, Examination Boards have been greatly stimulated by the *Taxonomy*: sometimes the same categories are used to describe the performances required in different subjects, and sometimes the subject specialists have developed their own categories. For example, in addition to knowledge, application, analysis and synthesis, the examination for Geometrical and Engineering Drawing (Joint Matriculation Board) includes:

Technique. The ways and means of using drawing instruments to achieve good draughtsmanship, well-proportioned sketches as well as constructional accuracy. (Example: ability to construct an accurate funicular polygon.)

Visualization and Interpretation. The demonstration of basic understanding of form and function from verbal or geographical information; translation of written information into drawings and vice versa; recognition of functional and dimensional requirements. (Examples: (a) ability to construct a cam profile from a descriptive specification; (b) ability to explain the functioning of a value from its assembly drawing.)

There are many other ways of deriving operational objectives of this kind, as for example from the task analysis of the jobs people do (see Youngman *et al*, 1978).

References

M Ainscow and D A Tweddle (1979) *Preventing Classroom Failure: An Objectives Approach*. London: Wiley.

W A L Blyth *et al* (1975) *Place, Time and Society 8-13: An Introduction*. Bristol: Collins.

L Cohen and N Garner (1971) *A Student's Guide to Teaching Practice*. London: London University Press.

L Cohen and L Mannion (1977) *A Guide to Teaching Practice*. London: Methuen.

W F Cone (1972) A teaching technique to increase teacher productivity, *Journal of Engineering Education*, 63, 180-1.

E J Furst (1960) *Constructing Evaluation Instruments*. New York: McKay.

R M Gagné (1976) *The Conditions of Learning*. New York: Holt, Rinehart and Winston.

J Heywood (1974) *Assessment in History*. Dublin: School of Education, University of Dublin.

J Heywood (1976) *Assessment in Mathematics*. Dublin: School of Education, University of Dublin.

J Heywood (1978) *Examining in Second Level Education*. Dublin: Association of Secondary Teachers, Ireland.

J Heywood, S McGuiness and D E Murphy (1981) *Final Report of the Public Examinations Evaluation Project to the Minister for Education*. Dublin: School of Education, University of Dublin.

Liberal Learning at Alverno College. Milwaukee, Wisconsin: Alverno College.

F J McDonald (1968) *Educational Psychology*. Belmont, Cal: Wadsworth.

J MacNamara and G Madaus (1970) *Public Examinations*. Dublin: Government Publications.

M B Youngman, R Oxtoby, J D Monk and J Heywood (1978) *Analysing Jobs*. Farnborough: Gower Press.

9 Appraisal and Self-appraisal

9.1 Introduction

The purpose of this final chapter is to look at two important concepts which relate to the professional performance of teachers. These concern the appraisals which teachers make of pupils as a guide both to perform-ance and teaching, and the appraisals which teachers ought to make of themselves. The appraisals which teachers make through examinations and tests are a relatively well explored territory (Heywood, 1978) whereas the idea of self-appraisal or self-evaluation is relatively new. Both involve graded answers to questions which relate to the performance of teachers in the classroom.

Sections 9.2—9.9 deal with appraisal of pupils in the classroom; section 9.10 looks at self-appraisal.

9.2 For whom

Appraisals of pupils are required for numerous purposes. All examinations and assessments have numerous functions. Broadly speaking however, there are four main users: parents, pupils, potential employers and teachers. They are concerned with the measurement of achievement, diagnoses of learning difficulties and the prediction of potential. Sometimes these functions are combined: an achievement test may be used to predict potential as well as to diagnose faults.

There is much confusion in the teaching community about the functions of tests and their ability to attain the goals demanded by those functions. Many teachers have criticized examinations because they depend on one day's performance, and that might be an off-day. Moreover, if they are badly designed they may test knowledge alone. For this reason, these teachers have advocated continuous assessment, that is, a series of tests set in class, from which is derived the overall grade at the end of the course. However, the effect may be no better and possibly worse than the effect of a public examination; often teachers set tests which assess the same limited skills. If essays are set for tests and homework it is unlikely that the reliability (see below) of the teacher' marking will be any different from that of the markers in a public examination; teachers must exercise the same amount of care.

There are two kinds of potential employer: those in the world of work and those in academia. There is an increasing trend for more adolescents to demand higher or further education. There is plenty of evidence to show that public examinations are useful predictors of those who are likely to succeed on academic courses. They do not indicate who will get the highest or the lowest grades; but they do give some indication as to who will pass and who will fail. They are unlikely to be replaced although the age level at which they become important may change as more and more pupils lengthen their education. Moreover, most examining authorities have tried to improve their techniques with multiple-strategy tests which give a profile of the significant learning skills required in the subject. At the moment the results are reported as a single grade. But there is increasing interest in the idea of presenting the results in the form of a profile (see Chapter 8 of Heywood, 1978). This, it is thought, may help employers and also assist teachers to devise courses for the less able which emphasize skills and qualities likely to be of value in work and life.

Both teachers and parents need to know much more about pupils if their appraisals are to be effective. The parent may often have a key role to play in remediation. Parents may also have justifiable complaints about their children's performance. Often children fail to learn with a teacher because of a poor interpersonal relationship. It should also be remembered that the parents of bright children will be as concerned for their perform-ance as the parents of the less able. Often, the brighter child will tend towards introversion, and some will suffer from study difficulties and pre-examination strain. The findings on student behaviour in higher education apply to the older adolescent (Malleson, 1966; Ryle, 1969).

Teachers will often be helped with their diagnoses if they know some-thing about the child's background. An altogether different profile require-ment emerges. If it takes into account the findings of educational research it becomes most detailed, as the example in Appendix 1 shows. Unfortu-nately, few teachers would feel competent to make the judgements which these profiles call for, though they often find themselves forced to make such evaluations. It is not the intention of this book to assist student teachers to develop these skills except insofar as their inspection of the profiles in the affective domain leads them to appreciate both the require-ments of the profile and the need for objectivity. The design of classroom assessments of attainment is part of lesson planning and implementation.

9.3 The criterion of assessment

The first criterion is objectivity. Formal assessments prevent us from relying on our impressions. The chapter on perception (Chapter 4) warns of the impressions gained from the judgements that are forced on us while we interact with a class. We require judgements that are both reliable and valid. Reliability means that if a test is repeated on a similar population (in respect of age, intelligence, background etc) it will produce a similar result. Validity means that it tests what it sets out to test. For example, if its purpose is to test the skill of analysis, multiple-choice questions designed to test the recall of knowledge are unlikely to test the skill of analysis.

9.4 Oral questioning

(a) Organizing question

What purposes are served by classifying the types of questions asked by teachers? Give examples, preferably from your own experience, of ways in which questioning strategies may be used to foster the achievement of learning objectives.

(b) Commentary

All tests require answers to questions. Oral questioning is the most often used classroom strategy. Teachers usually realize the potential of questioning, yet it can have consequences which the teacher does not realize. For example:

> In my first-year maths class I was very surprised when a normally very well behaved boy asked me what appeared to be a very rude question. He asked 'Why are teachers so stupid?' When I expressed mild shock at such a question from him he supplied the explanation which justified that his question was of a humorous nature rather than being rude. He continued by saying 'because you're always asking *us* questions about how to do the work!' I now discover that my purely instinctive action of teaching by using the questioning technique to a large extent, is in fact in accordance with teaching theory, and feel grateful for the reinforcement which the boy in class gave me.

The same student listed many of the well-known axioms about correct questioning:

1. Keep them from being long winded — avoid ambiguity.
2. The correct answer should be within the grasp of the pupils' intellect and knowledge.
3. Avoid changing the question if, often initially, nobody could answer it.
4. Avoid asking a string of questions without waiting for the answer to the first one.
5. Unless a certain pupil is named, have a clear, well-known system of who is to answer the question, ie avoid everyone shouting out the answer, eg hands up system could be used.
6. Avoid rhetorical questions (you might get the answer!).
7. Determine whether your questioning is to be:
   (a) *unstructured* — a non-behavioural response being sought, allowing the pupil much freedom of expression in answering.
   (b) *structured* — requiring a specific response to the question.
   (c) *highly structured* — requiring a very specific response which is usually a very clear cut answer being either right or wrong.
8. Avoid asking a question and then immediately answering it yourself before the class have sufficient time to propose an answer.

9. Avoid cutting answers short with a curt 'no'.

Mills distinguishes between questions which will make a class think and those which will test and confirm knowledge. If we want to set questions which will stimulate interest we will try to set puzzles or give quizzes. However, if we wish to make them think while a body of knowledge is constructed, we will try to arrange the questions so that a series of logical steps are taken. When, on the other hand, we are testing for knowledge, we may be aiming at feedback to show successes and failures in learning, or we may be revising in preparation for the next step.

It is important that teachers respond to questions. Pupils must know when they are 'right' and when they are 'wrong'. Reinforcement of a 'correct' response is helped by a simple reward 'That is right, good'. However, the pupil who is 'wrong' should not be chastised. Rather, he should be shown the correct response. It may be necessary to give the answer yourself, but you may feel there is time to help the child to work it out with you or to ask other children to provide the answer. In any event, it is essential to see that the child understands the answer. Children must not be made to feel foolish. Apart from their embarrassment in the class, they are likely to react against you in the future.

Giving a view of recent research, one respondent wrote:

> It is estimated that 60 per cent of a teacher's questions are of the lower order, data recall level; 20 per cent are procedural; and only 20 per cent are higher order. It has been shown that student teachers tend to jump too quickly to higher order questions, without building a lower order foundation — thus losing much of their 'audience'. Questions should follow a logical low → high sequence. It has also been shown that many teachers, particularly the inexperienced, do not leave enough 'answering' time.

Another research was described thus:

> One interesting study asked lower order questions to one group and higher order questions to another group after the same lesson — the latter group did better on a test immediately following the lesson than did the former group. The test was divided into a hierarchy of skills. Both groups performed similarly on lower order skills, but the second group did better on higher order skills.

The lower and higher order skills to which these responses refer are those of the Bloom *Taxonomy of Educational Objectives* described in Chapter 8. Most questions, it seems, seek to test whether the pupil remembers this or that, or whether he understands what is recalled. They do not, by and large, seek to test whether he can make judgements about controversies, or whether he can bring several ideas into a new synthesis, or analyse a passage of literature, an article from a newspaper or a scientific problem. It might be objected that this is not possible with junior classes, but there is a level of reasoning at which pupils in the younger age groups of second level education can demonstrate these skills. A more substantial objection may be that such questioning may take up too much time. But how can pupils learn if they are not shown how to discuss problems with the development of these skills in mind?

Possibly teachers think questioning is easy. Any teacher who has experienced microteaching programmes (Brown, 1975) designed to develop skills in questioning will know that such is not the case. Because they think it is easy they may not plan for the questions they wish to ask. So they generate a question in the class against a fixed perception of the answer. For example, one trainee teacher who was seeking the term 'excommuni-cation' rejected the term 'expel' out of hand. The same teacher spent 10 minutes trying to drag the term 'excommunication' out of the class without realizing that they had no prior knowledge of the term. He did not know when to stop, and as a result much time was lost. Effective questioning demands careful planning.

One of the most difficult skills in questioning is the selection of pupil respondents. It is not an easy task to be fair and ensure that each of 30 or so pupils are drawn into the questioning. At the very least, it is important to ensure that you do not continually select the same three or four pupils. There are one or two classrooms in higher education which are fitted with a microcomputer. Each desk has a set of buttons. When the teacher asks a question requiring 'yes/no' responses or a choice from five items, every student presses the button on his or her desk corresponding to the right answer. The teacher can see at once on his video screen who has the right answer and who has the wrong answer.

9.5 Testing and listening

The following response requires no comment:

> I believe that questioning is a form of listening. We form meaningful
> questioning sequences when we *listen* attentively — I believe that
> teachers should be trained in listening, in group work and in self
> development. If teachers could stop and listen, then I think that
> questions could be made more useful and more relevant.

9.6 Classroom testing

Classroom and homework tests often suffer the same fate as questioning: they are not sufficiently thought out and so their full potential is not realized. Like questions, they often only attempt to test recall of knowledge, but they can be used to do much more than this.

One reason why tests and questions may not be fully exploited is the desire of the teacher to cover the syllabus. To achieve this goal all the principles of learning are ignored in the chase for knowledge of facts, ie knowledge at the first level of the *Taxonomy*. Everything suffers. But an evaluation of the syllabus in terms of the concepts, principles and problems to be solved should cause the teacher to pause. Another reason is that teachers are not trained to design tests. Neither is it appreciated that pupils can also be trained with benefit to the development of their learning skills.

There is no space to deal fully with test construction: this is a specialist task and considered in detail in Heywood (1978). Nevertheless, some hints may be worthwhile.

Tests can be used in summative and formative modes of evaluation. As the 'sum-' implies, summative judgements are for the purpose of terminal or final judgements. More often than not, they are norm-referenced, ie they attempt to differentiate between the pupils in a group, as for example in public examinations. A formative judgement is one that is made *en passant*, while the pupil is *en route*. It is criterion-referenced. With its results the teacher can form judgements about a particular pupil since the criteria are stated with that purpose in mind. Some public examinations contain a combination of criterion- and norm-referenced tests. A project which is assessed for the skills shown in the report (and/or artefact) is criterion-referenced. In this sense a test of skills in driving is criterion-referenced. Good examples of criterion-referenced assessments are in the profiles in Appendix 1. Such tests will assist us in drawing up a pupil profile. More often than not, classroom tests are norm-referenced.

It is also necessary in the planning of classroom tests to distinguish between competency and mastery learning tests. A competency test seeks to examine very precisely defined skills. The driving test or examinations in flying are examples. But drivers and pilots have to pass these tests with a high level of competence. If they did not, they would constitute a menace. They need to have mastered the skills, hence the term 'mastery'. In programmed instruction the pupil does not proceed to the next section of work until he has mastered the first section. Pupils cannot proceed until they understand: even with a class of very bright pupils, this may mean that they have to learn at differential rates and, as we saw in Chapter 6, this poses considerable problems for the teacher. But it is the insistence on the same pace that often creates problems in classes and leads to unfair judgements of 'bright' and 'dull'.

9.7 Marking

Very often pupils do not benefit from the marks given for tests or home-work because the teacher does not feel it necessary to comment on the returned exercise or the class test. Many pupils have great difficulty in writing essays, whether of the imaginative, narrative or reasoning kind; and generally, it seems, pupils are inadequately trained in essay-writing. Class-room training can be provided, and it is possible that it will be enhanced by relating it to a mark scheme. This should have the advantage of sharpening the pupils' perception about what is wanted by examiners. But they cannot be shown on the mark scheme without explanation. Moreover, the remarks on the returned scripts need to be related to the scheme. I have used the scheme in Exhibit 3.2 with older pupils to great effect. Notice how it emphasizes skills. It is by no means perfect, and sometimes other descriptions may have to be placed alongside and in addition to the categories. There is no simple answer to the problem. In this particular case the schedule is aimed to test a candidate's skill in developing a logical argument. Many bright pupils go through school without learning the skills which will help them to do this. Specific training is required in the skills of learning.

9.8 Tests

It is not possible to deal with the subject of testing in a single section. At the same time, a few words on the pitfalls and potentials of classroom testing are appropriate.

All that has been said about questioning applies to testing. Very often all that is tested is knowledge. More often than not a test is threatened but, although it is given a week or so later, it is prepared at the last possible minute. Sometimes teachers say that they will test one thing and then test another. Often this creates stress and fear. Like lessons and questioning, tests need to be carefully planned.

If knowledge is being tested, items (questions) in the multiple-choice format are ideal. First, they provide a single solution; second, if the answer sheet is carefully designed they can be scored with a template; third, they are reliable; fourth, they can test a wide range of content in a relatively short period of time; and fifth, they can be evaluated for reliability and discrimination so that they can be stored for future use with similar groups of pupils. The technique of evaluation is called item analysis; most books on objective testing give simple formulae for the determination of discrimination among a group of pupils. An item which does not discriminate is discarded. Discrimination is a measure of the way in which the class respond to an item. For a good item it would be expected that 60 per cent or so of the pupils would get the answer right. The other 40 per cent think the other options are correct. Usually there are three or four options in addition to the answer. These are designed so that they 'appear' to be the correct answer. Suppose, in a four option item, 60 per cent got the answer right and the other 40 per cent chose one of the other options. Two would not be 'working' since no one chose them.

A good question will attract some pupils to respond to each of the items. Thus, while multiple-choice tests are an ideal way of testing a class, much time is spent in their design. Many books (subject-related) have been published with examples of such tests in second level education. But they do not (in general) give statistical data. If you use them you will have to undertake your own item analyses. The various forms of multiple objective items are shown in Exhibit 9.1. They do not only test recall of knowledge: for example, problem-solving skills will be used in the solution of many items set in mathematics. There are other ways of testing reasoning as Exhibit 9.2 shows. But assertion-reason questions are difficult to design

1. *Simple multiple-choice item with terminology shown*

STEM

Which one of the following is the primary purpose for which craft guilds were founded in the middle ages?

OPTIONS

Key

Distractors

A. The regulation of production

B. The distribution of goods
C. The control of town governments
D. The training of new workmen

2. *Multiple completion question*

In completing a project in school, in which order would you carry out the following steps:

(i) obtain evidence
(ii) formulate hypotheses
(iii) suggest a solution
(iv) analyse the data
(v) define the issue (problem)?

A. (ii), (v), (iv), (i), (iii)
B. (v), (ii), (i), (iv), (iii)
C. (iv), (v), (i), (iii), (ii)
D. (i), (iv), (ii), (v), (iii)
E. (v), (i), (ii), (iv), (iii)

3. *Matching items*

From the list of names below write the name of the person responsible for each of the following:

the first person to derive the mathematical laws
of the motion in the solar system   A or B or C or D or E

the first person to describe a statistical approach
to the analysis of human heredity   A or B or C or D or E

the first person to make a direct determination
of the gravitational constant   A or B or C or D or E

A. Cavendish
B. Galton
C. Kepler
D. Mendel
E. Newton

Exhibit 9.1 *Examples of objective items*

1. *Statements and their qualifications (true/false items)*

   Statement

   The total resistance in a
   DC electrical circuit is equal
   to the sum of the individual
   resistances

   Qualification

   when the resistances are
   connected in series.

   True/False

2. *Assertion/reason items*

   Which of the following is true of the statement below?

   A. Both statements are true and the reason is a correct explanation
      of the first statement.
   B. Both statements are true but the reason is not a correct explanation
      of the first statement.
   C. The first statement is true but the second is false.
   D. The first statement is false but the second is true.
   E. Both statement and reason are false.

   Assertion

   The acceleration of the moon
   away from the centre of the   *because*
   earth is

   $$\left(\frac{4\pi^2}{Tm^2} \right) d$$

   where d is the distance
   between the earth and the
   moon, and Tm is the time
   for one complete
   revolution.

   Reason

   Gravity decreases at a rate
   which is inversely proportional
   to the square of the distance
   from the centre of the earth.

Exhibit 9.2 *Types of true/false item*

and pupils require training in their handling. Assessment techniques and educational objectives are related. The more precise the objectives the more apparent the technique. For example if the pupils are to be trained to evaluate different sources about the same historical event, it will be necessary to design a test in which they are given time to read different source materials before being questioned about their relative contribution to our understanding of the historical event which is in focus.

Some learning outcomes will be better evaluated in course work, as for example in the design, planning and implementation of science experiments. Many skills can be tested in this way and a profile of student performance can be constructed. They can also assist in the evaluation of performance in the cognitive and affective domain, as the two items below from a scheme for the evaluation of projects show:

1. Analysis is a preliminary step to arranging the material collected in a coherent pattern. It involves the selection of the most important and relevant points from the information assembled. In this light, the candidate has:

   (a) isolated important issues, factors or questions arising from his topic   4 marks
   (b) distinguished some important issues arising from his topic   3 marks
   (c) failed to distinguish relevant from irrelevant material and issues and important from unimportant material and issues   1 mark
   (d) made no attempt at analysis   0 mark

2. In relation to the resources and time available, the candidate has:

   (a) used them well throughout the project   3 marks
   (b) used them reasonably for much of the project   2 marks
   (c) failed to make reasonable use of them over significant periods of the project   1 mark
   (d) made little use of them throughout the project   0 mark

Notice how the first question is an expansion of the ideas in the marking scheme in Exhibit 3.2. It could equally well be used in the evaluation of an essay. Notice too how these descriptions can be used to help pupils improve their performance.

9.9 Pupil appraisal profiles

Schemes built up of questions of this kind are profiles of the learning skills required for performance in a subject. They should be of considerable interest to employers. Indeed, when subjects take into account learning skills and values as well as their knowledge and principles, it can be seen that there is no real conflict between a person's needs at work, and his need for a 'liberal' education.

Be that as it may, there is within the teaching profession considerable interest in profiles as a more valuable means of reporting than school reports. The demand is for simple systems. The profile in Appendix 1 would be regarded as too complex although I would argue that it is what must emerge from the findings of educational research.

First to report on an inquiry and first to market a profile was the Scottish Head Teachers Association. It is called the School Leaving Report. The example in their book (1977) includes three main sections: skills, subject/activity assessment, and other observations.

The skills are listening, reading, visual understanding, physical co-ordination, speaking, writing, use of number and manual dexterity. Each one of these incorporates four statements. Thus under listening we read:

- ☐ acts independently and intelligently on complex verbal instructions
- ☐ can interpret and act on most complex instructions
- ☐ can interpret and act on straightforward instructions
- ☐ can carry out simple instructions with supervision.

A to D gradings are used, each letter representing approximately 25 per cent of the year group in each case. The similarity with items used for project assessment is marked. However, in this case the items range more widely over the total activity of learning behaviour whereas the project assessments are more intense and more related to specific subject areas.

The subject/activity assessment shows the number of years studied, achievement, enterprise (includes flair and creativity) and perseverance. Points, not remarks, are given for each of these areas. The potential that these reports have for the education of the less able seems to be considerable, and if they come into widespread use both teachers and employers will need to develop entirely new skills if profiles are to provide better interpretations than hitherto. It is also clear that many changes will have to be made in syllabuses and teaching if there is to be a successful development of these skills.

One course which attempts to achieve these kinds of change is the City and Guilds Vocational Preparation (General) 365 course. Its profile form is detailed. It tries to assess the following 14 abilities:

Social abilities	(1) working with colleagues, (2) working with others, (3) self-awareness
Communication	(4) talking and listening, (5) reading and writing, (6) visual understanding
Practical and numerical abilities	(7) using equipment, (8) dexterity and co-ordination, (9) measuring, (10) calculating
Decision-making abilities	(11) planning, (12) information seeking, (13) coping with problems, (14) evaluating results.

Each of these is assessed against four descriptions, as in the Scottish Head Teachers' profile. Thus for the ability of evaluating results, the four points are:

175

☐ can identify others' difficulties and so help to improve group
performance
☐ can assess own performance and identify possible improvements
☐ can assess own output for routine tasks independently
☐ can assess own results with guidance. Asks for advice.

On the report forms are spaces for examples of the student's work in each
of the 14 areas. Also included in the profile is a competency certificate
in the areas of career planning, world of work, understanding society,
economic understanding and environmental understanding. These state
whether or not the student has completed some or all of 18 tasks. For
example, a tick is put in a box if the student 'has investigated the basic
economic factors involved in running a business'.

The debate about profiles is only in its infancy. Much more will be
heard about them in the future. We may hope that this debate will, at the
very least, lead to an improvement in school reporting.

9.10 Self-appraisal: reporting on ourselves

The adoption of an objectives approach to curriculum planning implies that
both institutions and teachers will want to evaluate their work. The former
will do it with public accountability in mind, the latter for themselves, so
exercising professional accountability. Teachers must 'want' to test their
ideas and evaluate their courses. Some will want the full treatment of an
independent evaluator, others will want to use a consultant and help with
tests and computing, while some will want to do it themselves. Some
efforts may be good, some may be bad, but some action, however crude,
is surely better than nothing.

Interest in the subject of self-evaluation has increased in recent years.
Investigations of a Parliamentary Select Committee in the House of
Commons in the late 1970s began to talk about the need for institutions
to be publicly accountable. The idea was also thought about in the context
of schools and schoolteachers. Elliott (1976) refuted the American model
in which tests are used to assess very simple objectives. He argued that
schools should be responsible for their own self-evaluation, and discussed
how teachers could monitor their own performance. Some years earlier,
Cox and Boyson (1973) had argued, in contrast, for public accountability
with external control.

Meanwhile the number of papers and articles published on the topic
has merited the publication of three volumes of Bibliography and
Commentary (Elliott, 1980 and 1981). Local education authorities have
become interested in the problem and fairly sophisticated schemes for
the evaluation of primary schools have been developed (see Elliott,
Volume 3). While the subject is new, it is too large for any comprehensive
discussion here. However, it is a concept which should not escape the
student teacher, for if in future years he or she fails to evaluate his or her
performance that performance is unlikely to retain the enthusiasm of

earlier years. More positively, without an adaptable and flexible teaching community the curriculum will not respond to the changing patterns of knowledge which will be imposed on us by changing technology. We ought always to review our practice and be prepared to invite observers into our lessons.

Yates (1981), a headmaster writing in Volume 3 of Elliott's bibliography, said:

> Of course, it must be true to say that there are very few teachers who do not, to some extent, reflect on their effectiveness as teachers. Even the most insensitive must ask themselves from time to time how successful they are proving to be. Most of us ask ourselves, 'How did the lesson go?' or 'Was that really the best way of dealing with that child or that problem?' We also ask ourselves more long term questions, 'Are my methods of teaching spelling proving successful?' or 'Is my classroom manner as positive and encouraging as it might be?' Schools as a whole are similarly concerned to know how well they are achieving their aims: teachers come together, formally and informally, to discuss problems and perhaps find solutions. What I suggest to you is that the type of self-evaluation at present taking place in schools, certainly in mine, is far too unsystematic and unplanned for present needs. The problem is not that teachers are insufficiently self-critical — the truth is that many are too self-critical — but that they do not organize themselves sufficiently in this respect and do not form strategies for self-evaluation either as individuals or groups. We need to spend much more time asking ourselves *why* we do what we do and getting together as school staffs to look critically at schemes and policies.

Until that happens the student is on his or her own. The teacher, as Habershaw (1980) points out, has to become responsible for himself and his development. In terms of Maslow's theory of motivation (see Chapter 2) appraisal should lead the teacher to self-actualization: thus the student teacher profile (Appendix 2) becomes a teacher profile. In the first year or so, the teacher's concern is likely to be with his or her own planning and performance. Pope and Keen (1981) have shown how personal constructs may be used by trainee teachers for self-appraisal. But if, like the profiles in Appendix 2, they are thought to be too difficult, then a simpler checklist might be modified for use on an annual basis.

As an example, we conclude this book with Roberts' scheme of lesson evaluation which is used in the training of graduates for teaching at the City of Liverpool College of Higher Education (Roberts, 1982). It can be turned into a scheme which will evaluate a year's work. In the absence of any opportunity for systematic evaluation in the school, the teacher might write himself a letter which takes into account his overall performance during the year against those headings.

A SCHEME FOR SELF-EVALUATION

The purpose of evaluation is to determine how much the behaviour of the children has changed at the completion of the activity. To be effective it needs to be continuous — as an integral part of the teacher-learning process, from lesson to lesson and day to day. It is the only basis upon which teaching methods can be modified and improved.

It means critically examining not only the educational outcome of a lesson or series of lessons but comparing them with the expected outcomes and then judging whether, how and where changes should be made, if any.

So we need to look closely at —

(a)   the aims and/or objectives as defined at the outset
(b)   the content of what was taught
(c)   the method by which it was taught.

so that learning experiences can be presented in the most effective and enjoyable way.

Aspects to be considered after completing a lesson, topic or scheme of work:

A. *PLANNING*

   (i)   Were the most appropriate objectives identified?
  (ii)   How accurate was my assessment of the children's background knowledge, interests and abilities?
 (iii)   Were the most appropriate resources prepared and made available beforehand?
 (iv)   Was a proper balance of activities planned to allow for active participation by the children and a variety of activity during the longer periods?
  (v)   Did I choose the best method of approach?
 (vi)   Did I have adequate knowledge of the subject matter?

B. *INTRODUCTION*

  (i)   Was the Introduction suited to the development of the activity?
 (ii)   Was it too long or not long enough?
(iii)   Was the purpose of the lesson made clear to the children?
(iv)   Did all the children understand what to do, what to read, how they should record their work and what standards to achieve?
 (v)   Would a demonstration have helped the development along by improving understanding of what was expected in it?

C. *DEVELOPMENT*

   (i)   Was the content suited to the intellectual development and experience of the children?
  (ii)   Was the lesson material well organized and, if necessary, prepared well beforehand?
 (iii)   Was appropriate emphasis placed upon meaning and the important details of the lesson?
 (iv)   How effectively were correlations made with other subjects, if any?
  (v)   Were the blackboard, workcards, text and reference books used to the best advantage?
 (vi)   Were the appropriate visual aids used — and how effectively?

Evaluation (continued)

(vii) Did all groups/individuals get a fair share of attention and guidance — by helping children to help themselves, by diagnosing group/individual weaknesses, and by applying the most appropriate remedial measures where necessary?

(viii) Were the children allowed to participate actively in the lesson or were they passively receptive?

(ix) Was any discussion guided so that everyone got some satisfaction from it?

(x) Were questions well worded, well distributed, in logical sequence?

(xi) How successful was I in dealing with incorrect or partial answers?

(xii) Was interest maintained throughout the activity or was restlessness and boredom obvious?

(xiii) Was the noise excessive in view of the type of work being carried out?

D. *CONCLUSION*

(i) Was the work involved related to the development or given merely to occupy the children? Was it specific, or vague and general?

(ii) Was sufficient time allowed for the children to complete the set work?

(iii) Was suitable provision made for those children who completed their work well within the allotted period?

(iv) Was the stage set for further learning? How much revision will be necessary; who will need it; how will it be carried out?

(v) What will be the next stage? Were the children interested or knowledgeable enough to continue with the activity with understanding or will a change of method and/or subject matter be necessary?

E. *CONTROL*

(i) How successful was I in winning the children's co-operation and in establishing good work habits?

(ii) Were the routine duties and activities carried out with the minimum of supervision?

(iii) How effective was I in dealing promptly, quietly and firmly with misconduct?

F. *PERSONAL QUALITIES*

(i) Was I relaxed, tense, or nervous?

(ii) Was my voice suitably loud, properly pitched, and did it have suitable inflexion?

(iii) Was the rate of speech satisfactory and did it vary according to circumstances?

(iv) Was my vocabulary suited to the children's understanding? Did I talk down to them?

(v) Did I listen to the children?

(vi) Did I show a sense of humour whilst still maintaining control?

Exhibit 9.3 *Evaluation*
(from Roberts, 1982; reproduced with his permission)

References

G Brown (1975) *Microteaching: A Programme of Teaching Skills.* London: Methuen.

C B Cox and R Boyson (eds) (1973) *The Accountability of Schools: An Analysis of Present Trends in Education and Suggestions to Make Schools More Responsive to External Standards and Parental Choice.* Enfield: National Council for Educational Standards.

G Elliott (1980-81) *Self Evaluation and the Teacher: An Annotated Bibliography and Report on Current Practice*, Volumes 1, 2 and 3. Hull: University of Hull/Schools Council.

J Elliott (1976) Preparing teachers for classroom accountability, *Education for Teaching*, 100, 49-72.

T Habershaw (1980) Towards a system of continuing self-development for teachers, *British Journal of Educational Technology*, 11, 48-54.

J Heywood (1977) *Assessment in Higher Education.* London: Wiley.

J Heywood (1978) *Examining in Second Level Education.* Dublin: ASTI.

N Malleson (1966) *British Student Medical Health Services.* London: Pitman.

H W Mills (1972) *Teaching and Training: A Handbook for Instruction.* New York: Macmillan.

M L Pope and T R Keen (1981) *Personal Construct Psychology and Education.* London: Academic Press.

R F Roberts (1982) *Preparation for Teaching Practice.* Liverpool: City of Liverpool College of Higher Education.

A Ryle (1969) *Student Casualties.* London: Allen Lane/Penguin.

Scottish Head Teachers Association (1977) *Pupils in Profile.* London: Hodder and Stoughton.

M Yates (1981) Self-evaluation in the primary school, in G Elliott (ed) *Self Evaluation and the Teacher*, Volume 3. Hull: University of Hull/Schools Council.

Note:
A similar scheme to Roberts' but related to an annual review is by Joan Dean (1980) Time to take stock, in *Junior Education*, Summer 1980.

Appendix 1: Experimental Pupil Evaluation Form for Teachers

Below is given part of The Pupil Evaluation Form by D E Murphy,* modified and developed from the method of assessment of medical practitioners developed by Byrne and Hodgkins with the assistance of J Freeman (see J Freeman and P S Byrne (1973) *The Assessment of Post-Graduate Training in General Practice.* Guildford: Society for Research into Higher Education).

Section A

Criterion 1: Knowledge

Knowledge involves the recall of the idea or phenomenon in a form very close to that in which it was originally encountered by the pupil.

Negative:
The pupil follows no routine of work or questioning the teacher in class. He fails to identify and does not bother to develop salient leads. He will not pursue alternative hypotheses. He does not seek information. His written work is sketchy and not systematic. He tends to investigate in a haphazard fashion.

Positive:
The pupil has a routine of work and is comprehensive in his work and questioning of the teacher in class and outside class if he gets the opportunity. His investigations particularly in pursuing a project are intelligently and economically planned. He records his information carefully and uses previous and continuing knowledge intelligently. He plans investigations and inquiries.

Criterion 2: Problem finding

Problem finding ability is necessary when the pupil is expected to examine critically data presented to him, eg an historical account or description.

---

* First published in *Assessment in History (Twelve to Fifteen)* (1974) pp 162-70. Report No 1 of the Public Examinations Evaluation Project, Dublin: School of Education, University of Dublin. (Abbreviated version; the 12-point scales with each profile are omitted.)

Negative:
This pupil cannot see various contradictions which may be in a text or narrative. He accepts what is written on the external authority of the author alone without looking for an intrinsic logic and consistency in the passage or account.

Positive:
This pupil is reasonably demanding and critical of what is given by the teacher and of what is written in various textbooks. He is sensitive to what may be propagandistic approaches in history or literature and is quick to realize an instance in which there is illogicality or intrinsic contradiction in material he has to study.

Criterion 3: Problem solving

Problem solving is concerned with the pupil's ability and skill in using information gained to develop judgement.

Negative:
The pupil does not fully realize the implications of the data which he collects. He is unable to interpret the unexpected result which he may often ignore, and his thinking tends to be rigid and unimaginative and impedes his recognition of associated problems. His general shortcomings – rigidity of thought and lack of capacity to be flexible or to diverge when thinking over a particular problem – have an inhibiting effect on his effectiveness.

Positive:
The pupil realizes the importance of unexpected findings and seeks to interpret them. He understands the nature of probability and uses this to assist his decision making. He takes all data into account before making a decision. He thinks effectively – he has the capacity to range flexibly or 'diverge' – in the search for relevant factors in connection with the particular problem in hand, and he has also the capacity to focus or 'converge' his thinking on whatever factors have been decided on as relevant.

Criterion 4: Transfer of learning

Application of knowledge and problem solving developed in the classroom in one subject to other subjects or to extra-curricular activities, such as the various school clubs or societies to which he may belong.

Negative:
The pupil is concerned with gaining knowledge and problem solving ability in the classroom but does not seem to see this as relevant to his other activities outside class. Seems unable to hold a serious or reasonable conversation. There is

Positive:
The pupil, without obviously trying to impress, shows signs that the knowledge he gains in the classroom and the problem solving experience he gets there overflows into his extra-curricular activities. His conversation is reasonable and

little or no evidence that his classroom experience influences his behaviour.

interesting. His general behaviour is consistent with his classroom disposition.

Criterion 5: Application of learning to personal relationships

Willingness and ability to cope with other pupils in the class and outside class in matters concerning school work or what he has learned indicates a maturity.

Negative:
This pupil is not prepared to discuss with his peers matters arising in the classroom. When given the opportunity by the teacher, he will not listen reasonably to them or debate with them. He has difficulty in understanding points raised by his peers or is intolerant of them. He may be discouraged by them or he himself may be overbearing towards them.

Positive:
This pupil is interested in contributions his classmates have to make. He is prepared to listen to them seriously and relate with them in academic discussion in class and outside class when the opportunity arises. The subject matter of the classroom seems to contribute towards the enriching of his relationship with others.

Criterion 6: Responsibility in learning

A sense of responsibility should be present in the pupil because knowledge, unless used properly, can become a deadweight contributing little or nothing positive to the pupil as a member of society.

Negative:
This pupil loses interest once he has grasped a point or if there is particular difficulty involved in some aspect of the subject matter in hand. He is careless about his presentation of set work. He is inclined to 'copy' and prone to 'artfully dodge' taking on anything over and above the minimum necessary for his own survival.

Positive:
This pupil has an interest in the subject and seems to appreciate its relevance to his general formation. He tends to ask the kind of questions which demonstrate his desire to use the subject matter in relation to what appear to be his current idealisms or interests. Is generous in any common projects and is serious about any tasks given to him by the teacher. Always tends to present his own work and take responsibility for it.

Criterion 7: Promptness in application of learning

The ability to respond quickly and accurately in various situations is a commendable feature in a pupil. It is inborn to some extent but it can also be developed to some extent.

Negative:
This pupil panics easily. He becomes confused under pressure and has difficulty in establishing priorities. He is unable or unwilling to make and sustain decisions alone. He cannot adequately adapt his knowledge to cope with a sudden or unexpected problem.

Positive:
This pupil quickly assesses a situation and establishes priorities with full regard to whatever procedures are necessary. Without being neurotic about it, he is aware of the value of quick response in certain situations. If necessary he is able to draw on knowledge from whatever source. He is able and willing to make and sustain decisions alone.

Criterion 8: Originality and creativity

Every pupil has something special of himself to bring to a subject which he is studying. A feature perhaps which is not always appreciated or understood and difficult to assess by means of any kind of general or objective testing.

Negative:
This pupil will be slow or unwilling to come forward with any ideas that he has not seen in a book or been given by the teacher. He will stick slavishly to repeating what he feels will please the teacher. He shows little imagination and he reveals little of himself in work presented or in his response in class.

Positive:
This pupil is bright and courageous in drawing and presenting his own reasonable conclusions about material concerning the subject being taught. Is imaginative in his presentation of work or in his general response in class. Is concerned with the truth as he understands it and is able to present an interesting perspective of this truth.

Section B

Criterion 1: Family background

Accepting that the teacher is *in loco parentis* in the education of the child, and the teacher's role is to complement the formative task of the parent, this criterion is concerned with the co-operation that you seem to get from the parents of this pupil.

Negative:
A pupil with unco-operative parents may not be supplied with the necessary learning materials. He may complain of not having facilities at home for doing any exercises you may give him.

Positive:
A pupil with co-operative parents will generally be supplied with recommended books and materials or if there are economic reasons why these are not forthcoming, adequate explanation will be

When there is a genuine reason for absences or for not being able to do his homework he may not be given an excuse by his parents. Physical appearance may be neglected.

made to the teacher in a way that will avoid any embarrassment to the child. Excuses will be respectfully submitted to the teacher when the child has been absent or unable to attend to his homework.

Criterion 2: Educational background

This criterion concerns the previous schooling of the pupil which should have been homogeneous with the approach of his teacher at second level.

Negative:
The teacher has not acquired or been given adequate information about the pupil's previous or primary school background. The pupil is not able to express himself with ease in the classroom. He seems to be afraid of his teacher. He has difficulty in writing and spelling properly.

Positive:
There is adequate liaison with the pupil's primary school. His primary school teacher still shows interest in him and would, if necessary, be prepared to talk helpfully about him. He has a good relationship with his present teacher. He can converse with ease and read and write properly.

Criterion 3: Moral environment

This criterion concerns the moral environment from which the child comes. The strictness or laxity of the parents in their own behaviour and in their approach to the behaviour of the child.

Negative:
The pupil comes from a home background which is either puritanical or moralistic or from a background in which there are no moral standards upheld. The pupil is not allowed to question reasonably any of the standards accepted by his parents. He is expected to comply unquestioningly with his parents' norms of behaviour. He is never expected to act reasonably.

Positive:
The pupil has parents who are concerned with him as a person, who respect his separateness and while anxious to transmit their standards in no way force them on him but encourage him to develop a critical faculty — accepting their standards not because they look on him as an extension of themselves without individuality, but as someone who must be encouraged to give real assent to their tenets. They seem to allow him to affirm his own individuality.

Criterion 4: Influence of school authorities

Concerns co-operation with teachers and pupils on the part of the principal of the school. The influence of a principal on the efficiency of teachers is great and a spirit of unity and co-operation in a school makes it into a real learning society.

Negative:

The principal is ever occupied with matters of material administration. He is inaccessible and even when consulted is patronizing or dictatorial. Shows little understanding of the learning process. Is more concerned with the 'good name' of the school than with individual pupils. Attempts at reasonable innovation are not favoured.

Positive:

The principal is obviously dedicated to managing the conditions of learning so as to provide an atmosphere of happiness for teachers and pupils. He is easy to relate to and shows empathy with teachers and pupils. Is committed to real progress in learning in the school.

Criterion 5: Emotional development

This criterion concerns the pupil's sexuality which has an important bearing on his ability to concentrate. At this particular time the boy or girl may be able to cope with adolescence or may be in turmoil.

Negative:

The pupil shows signs of withdrawal into himself. Is inclined to daydream. There is some indication that he is the victim of sexual exploitation by others. Asks questions in class which show a sexual naivety and unpreparedness. Is normally outgoing but inclined to get particularly embarrassed or inclined to withdraw into himself when anything concerning reproduction arises in any context. Is sexually precocious. Asks questions which indicate no parental help in working through adolescent anxieties.

Positive:

The pupil demonstrates an ease with his own body. Has a vocabulary wherewith he can talk about matters concerning sexuality which may easily arise in any class situation. Shows no signs of undue anxiety and is alert, not usually given to withdrawal and daydreaming. Shows indications that his parents are making every effort to guide him through adolescence.

Criterion 6: Physical health

This criterion concerns the physical health of the pupil which is important for the teacher to know about, particularly because concentration in class and general interest may be impaired due to ill health which may not be apparent.

Negative:

No statement about the health of the pupil has been made to the

Positive:

The health of the pupil has been stated as good. The teacher is teacher. There seems to be some possibility that the pupil is in pain or physically embarrassed on occasion. There is a likelihood that hearing/sight are deficient in some way. The pupil has an obvious deformity which he seems unable to cope with.

reasonably certain that the pupil has no toilet problems. Hearing and sight are acute. Physical appearance is such that the pupil is comfortable with his class and teachers.

Criterion 7: Material facilities

Concerns the facilities available in the school. Adequate accommodation and the availability of necessary teaching materials make the transfer of learning most effective as a rule, making it possible for both teacher and pupil to be at their best in terms of dedication and receptivity.

Negative:
The building is inadequate. The classrooms are unsuitable, neglected, not properly cleaned, cold. Cloakroom and recreational facilities are inadequate. Reasonable teaching materials and aids not provided or come by only with great difficulty.

Positive:
The building is good and suitable for educational purposes. Teaching materials and aids are available when necessary. The pupils have all necessary conveniences provided. The material provisions of the school are all that one might reasonably expect.

Appendix 2: Student Teacher Evaluation Form

Below is given the *Student Teacher Evaluation Form* developed by
D E Murphy for the Public Examinations Evaluation Project.* It is
suggested that you use these scales to check your progress during your
initial training whether you are a 'he' or a 'she'. The 12-point scales with
each profile have been omitted.

Criterion 1: Information gathering

This criterion is concerned with the student's willingness, ability and skill
in gathering information necessary for decisions.

Negative:

She follows no routine of inquiry
about each pupil. She fails to
identify or does not bother to
develop salient leads. She will not
pursue alternative hypotheses. Her
record taking is sketchy and not
systematic. She tends to use
investigation in a 'blunderbuss'
fashion. She will not have familiarity with previous history of
pupils concerning their classwork
and possible social or emotional
problems. She will not have made
an effort to get relevant information from previous teachers of
the pupils.

Positive:

She carefully gathers and records
useful information about each
pupil, and when appropriate includes psychological and social
factors. Her inquiries about the
pupil are intelligently and tactfully
carried out. When necessary she
records her information carefully
and uses previous and continuing
records intelligently. She plans
carefully any investigation she
wants to make about the pupil and
uses with discrimination various
sources of information.

Criterion 2: Problem solving

This criterion is concerned with the student's ability and skill in using
information available about the pupil in order to contribute more
effectively towards facilitating the learning processes of the pupil.

* J Heywood, S McGuinness and D Murphy (1980) *The Public Examinations
Evaluation Project: Final Report to the Minister for Education*. Dublin: University
of Dublin School of Education.

Negative:
She does not fully realize the implications of the data concerning the pupil which she possesses. She is unable to interpret the unexpected happening which she may then ignore. Her thinking tends to be rigid and unimaginative and impedes her recognition of associated problems. Her general shortcomings — rigidity of thought and lack of the capacity to be flexible when thinking over a particular problem — has an inhibiting effect on her effectiveness.

Positive:
She realizes the importance of various items of information which come to her notice about the pupil and seeks to interpret them. She takes all relevant data into account before making a decision and routinely tests alternative hypotheses. She thinks effectively. She has the ability to be flexible in searching for relevant factors in connection with the particular problem in hand and she also has the capacity to focus or converge her thinking on whatever factors have been decided upon as relevant.

Criterion 3: Judgement

This criterion is concerned with the student's ability to use sound judgement in planning for and conducting her classes and in putting her decisions into practice.

Negative:
She is concerned more with fulfilling details of the syllabus than in education. She plans for her pupils without the necessary background information. She is rigid in her ideas and tends to have set or favourite routines. She does not appear to inspire confidence in her pupils. She refuses to explain things to pupils when reasonably asked.

Positive:
She is familiar with the uses and limitations of methods she may select. She recognizes her own limitations. She shows regard for the individual pupil's needs, wishes and general circumstances. She will modify procedures or decisions when the situation requires that she should do so. She inspires confidence in her pupils and is ready to explain to them her proposals and procedures in accordance with their ability to understand.

Criterion 4: Relationships with pupils

This criterion is concerned with the student's general influence on her pupils.

Negative:
She does not relate well with pupils either through aloofness, discourtesy, indifference or

Positive:
She gives confidence to pupils, affords co-operation and relieves any anxieties that they may have.

189

pressure of work, concerning the material aspects of the classroom. She has difficulty in understanding her pupils' needs. She is unable to give pupils confidence and may even alarm them unnecessarily. She reacts poorly to a pupil's hostile or emotional behaviour. She does not exhibit sympathy or compassion in dealing with pupils.

While pupils appreciate her interest in their well-being, she herself does not become emotionally over-involved with them. She is honest with the pupil and with the pupil's parents. Pupils like her and seem to feel that she is the kind of person of whom they may ask questions or with whom they may discuss problems.

Criterion 5: Continuing responsibility

This criterion is concerned with the student's willingness to accept and fulfil the responsibility for the growth and development of the pupil over a long period.

Negative:

She loses interest after a short time. Does not spend time looking towards the general progress of her pupils. She becomes discouraged with slow progress in pupils and cannot cope with a class which seems to be getting nowhere. She uses ancillary or voluntary personnel inadequately, or demands greater assistance from them than they are really competent to give her. She fails to review the pupil's progress at suitable intervals.

Positive:

She encourages a pupil to work for the pupil's own advancement and demonstrates that she too has the same objective. She observes her pupils' progress and alters her management procedures as required. She understands the role of ancillary and voluntary personnel and makes maximum effective use of their help and assistance. She maintains a persistently positive attitude to education. Is prepared to furnish adequate information to others whom she thinks may help the pupil.

Criterion 6: Ability to cope with crises

This criterion is concerned with the student's ability to cope with situations which require quick thinking and discrimination.

Negative:

She panics easily and loses valuable time by ineffective action. She becomes confused under pressure and has difficulty in establishing priorities. She is unable to delegate appropriate aspects of care to others. She is unable or unwilling to make and sustain decisions alone.

Positive:

She quickly assesses a situation and establishes priorities. She is aware of consequences of delay and can judge with reasonable accuracy when a situation (eg a disciplinary problem or a physical or emotional problem of a particular pupil) is beyond her own ability to cope with. She is able to obtain and organize the assistance of others. She is able and willing to make and sustain decisions alone if necessary.

Criterion 7: Relationships with teacher colleagues

This criterion is concerned with the student's effectiveness in working with other teachers.

Negative:
She does not relate well with teachers, either through aloofness, discourtesy, indifference or pressure of work. She has difficulty in understanding other teachers' interests in the development of particular pupils or classes of pupils with which she herself is involved. She reacts poorly to the emotional or hostile behaviour of a colleague. She does not exhibit sympathy or understanding in her peer relationships.

Positive:
She co-operates with other teachers and has confidence in herself. She does not demonstrate any superiority or inferiority tendencies. She seems to be well thought of and is accepted seriously by other teachers. She is willing to take on extra work on occasion to help an overworked or sick colleague. She does not get upset easily by apparent shortcomings in other teachers. She is conscious of the need for teamwork. She seeks consultation when appropriate and respects the views of others.

Criterion 8: Relationship with authority

This criterion is concerned with the student's ability to work effectively with her school principal and/or manager.

Negative:
She does not have the ability to take instructions gracefully or she takes instructions in a robot fashion and unquestioningly when questions might show concern and interest in the instruction given — is sullenly obedient. She tends to be tactless and inconsiderate. She is unwilling to refer to authority when necessary. She has no sense of loyalty to the principal and/or management of the school.

Positive:
She listens intelligently and critically to instructions. She makes the decisions of higher authority her own before acting on them. She will gracefully voice disagreement when she has what seems to be a 'good case'. She seeks consultation when necessary and is appreciative of the interest shown by authority. She creates an atmosphere of 'working with' rather than 'working for' the authorities.

Criterion 9: Professional values

This criterion is concerned with the student's attitudes and standards as an individual member of the teaching profession.

Negative:

She tends to be incommunicative with colleagues or superiors about any teaching difficulties she may have. She is difficult to locate when her help may be needed. She does not make adequate or proper arrangements when she needs a deputy or substitute. She tends to discuss the faults of colleagues or of the school authorities with pupils. She will talk generally about superiors and colleagues in a destructive way and does not seem to have the courage or interest necessary to confront colleagues when necessary.

Positive:

She is kind, courteous and honest. She communicates accurately and well. She will talk about her own mistakes or professional problems with colleagues or superiors. She respects any confidence she may have from other teachers or from the school authorities or from the pupils. She places pupil care above personal considerations. She recognizes her own professional capabilities and limitations. She can recognize when a particular pupil is in need of special or remedial treatment.

Selected Bibliography

M Ainscow and D A Tweddle (1979) *Preventing Classroom Failure: An Objectives Approach*. London: Wiley.

E Belbin and R M Belbin (1977) *Retraining Adult Workers*. London: Heinemann.

R F Biehler (1978) *Psychology Applied to Teaching*. Boston, Mass: Houghton Mifflin.

J S Bruner (1971) *The Relevance of Education*. Harmondsworth: Penguin.

L Buxton (1981) *Do You Panic About Maths? Coping With Maths Anxiety*. London: Heinemann.

L Cohen and L Mannion (1977) *A Guide to Teaching Practice*. London: Methuen.

S J Eggleston (1977) *The Sociology of the Curriculum*. London: Routledge and Kegan Paul.

R E FitzGibbons (1981) *Making Educational Decisions: An Introduction to Philosophy of Education*. New York: Harcourt Brace Jovanovich.

R M Gagné (1976) *The Conditions of Learning* (3rd edition). New York: Holt, Rinehart and Winston.

D H Hamblin (1981) *Teaching Study Skills*. Oxford: Basil Blackwell.

M Herbert (1981) *Behavioural Treatment of Problem Children: A Practice Manual*. London: Academic Press.

J Heywood (1978) *Examining in Second Level Education*. Dublin: Association of Secondary Teachers, Ireland.

B Hopson and M Scally (1981) *Life Skills Teaching*. London: McGraw-Hill.

G B Matthews (1980) *Philosophy and the Young Child*. Cambridge, Mass: Harvard University Press.

J G Rawlinson (1981) *Creative Thinking and Brainstorming*. Aldershot: Gower Press.

M Saunders (1979) *Class Control and Behaviour Problems*. London: McGraw-Hill.

J Turner (1977) *Psychology for the Classroom*. London: Methuen.

K Weber (1982) *The Teacher is the Key: A Practical Guide for Teaching the Adolescent with Learning Difficulties*. Milton Keynes: Open University Press.

P Westwood (1975) *The Remedial Teachers' Handbook*. Edinburgh: Oliver and Boyd.

A N Whitehead (1932) *The Aims of Education*. London: Benn.

Name Index

Subject Index